TO THE
MOUNTAINTOP

CHARLAYNE HUNTER-GAULT

TO THE MOUNTAINTOP

MY JOURNEY THROUGH THE CIVIL RIGHTS MOVEMENT

A New York Times Book

SQUARE
FISH

ROARING BROOK PRESS
NEW YORK

To the Giants—known and unknown—who made my journey possible;
and to my children, Suesan and Chuma, and all the members of the Joshua Generation
and beyond who hopefully will "keep on keepin' on."

SQUARE
FISH

An Imprint of Macmillan
175 Fifth Avenue
New York, NY 10010
macteenbooks.com

Square Fish and the Square Fish logo are trademarks of Macmillan and
are used by Roaring Brook Press under license from Macmillan.

Square Fish books may be purchased for business or promotional use. For information on bulk
purchases, please contact the Macmillan Corporate and Premium Sales Department at
(800) 221-7945 x 5442 or by e-mail at specialmarkets@macmillan.com.

Library of Congress Cataloging-in-Publication Data
Hunter-Gault, Charlayne.
To the mountaintop: my journey through the civil rights movement / Charlayne
Hunter-Gault.
p.   cm.
Includes bibliographical references and index.
ISBN 978-1-250-04062-6 (paperback)
1. Hunter-Gault, Charlayne—Juvenile literature.   2. Journalists—United States—
Biography—Juvenile literature.   3. African American journalists—Biography—Juvenile
literature.   4. Civil rights movements—Southern States—History—20th century—Juvenile
literature.   5. Southern States—Race Relations—Juvenile literature.   6. African Americans—
Civil rights—Southern States—History—20th century—Juvenile literature.   I. Title.
PN4874.H83A3 2012   070.92—dc23   [B]   2011020894

Originally published in the United States by Roaring Brook Press
First Square Fish Edition: 2014
Book designed by Jay Colvin
Square Fish logo designed by Filomena Tuosto

1   3   5   7   9   10   8   6   4   2

AR: 9.3 / LEXILE: 670L

CONTENTS

"We've got some difficult days ahead. But it doesn't matter with me now. Because I've been to the mountaintop . . . And I've looked over. And I've seen the Promised Land."

—*Martin Luther King, Jr.*

RACIAL BARRIER FAL

ONLINE

*test state-by-state
the presidential contest
use, Senate and
rs' races.*

*aucus blog: updates
e Times's political staff.*

*ctive graphics: the
l map, voter profiles
lysis.*

*, audio and photos:
s from the voters and
paigns.*

.com

ESIDENT-ELECT

NG CAMPAIGN

ey to the Top

ry of Senator Barack
's journey to the pinnacle
rican politics is the story
paign that was, even in
v of many rivals, almost
s. After a somewhat lack-
tart, Mr. Obama and his

S IN DECISIVE VICTOR

Democrats in Co
Strengthen G

By ADAM NAGOURNEY

Barack Hussein Obama was electe
dent of the United States on Tuesday, sw
last racial barrier in American politics
country chose him as its first black chief

The election of Mr. Obama amount
catharsis — a repudiation of a historicall
publican president and his economic a
icies, and an embrace of Mr. Obama's ca
the direction and the tone of the country.

But it was just as much a striking
ment in the evolution of the nation's frau
ry, a breakthrough that would have seer
just two years ago.

Mr. Obama, 47, a first-term senator
feated Senator John McCain
of Arizona, 72, a former prisoner of war who was mak-
ing his second bid for the
presidency.

To the very end, Mr.
McCain's campaign was
eclipsed by an opponent
who was nothing short of a
phenomenon, drawing huge
crowds epitomized by the
tens of thousands of people
who turned out to hear Mr.
Obama's victory speech in Grant Park in

Mr. McCain also fought the head
lentlessly hostile political environment,
with the baggage left to him by Preside

INTRODUCTION

On January 20, 2009, 1.8 million people crowded onto the cold, hard grounds of the nation's capitol in Washington, D.C., to witness the swearing in of the first black president of the United States of America. Many had come throughout the night to make sure they would be able to get a spot in the audience. My husband, Ronald, and I had flown sixteen hours from our home in Johannesburg, South Africa. We chose to take our chances coming at the crack of dawn, snaking through the long tunnel with hundreds of high-spirited revelers to get to the security check-point and onto the grounds.

As the sun rose, a mostly clear blue sky promised a bright day, and the gathering took on the air of a gigantic picnic. We had managed to get seats about a third of the way back from the podium, but neither we nor anyone else sat down. We kept moving in order to keep our warm blood flowing, and watched in amazement the growing throngs stretching as far as the eye could see—from just beneath the

Facing page: 1.8 million people came to the swearing-in of the first black president at the Capitol in Washington, D.C., on January 20, 2009.

Previous pages: *The New York Times* front page from November 5, 2008. For full text of Obama article, see page 142.

podium where Barack Obama would soon step into history, all the way to the stately white marble Washington Monument, a few minutes' walk at a brisk pace.

My husband and I had made this long journey to witness what we believed would be one of the greatest moments of our lifetime. For me, it was the climax of an even longer journey, one that I had begun with thousands of others back in the late fifties and early sixties: the civil rights movement.

The inauguration was another milestone on the long walk to freedom from unjust laws and their unjust consequences. Activists in the movement, in one way or another, had set America on the path to this moment by demanding for black people the wholeness of citizenship: equality of opportunity. On that January morning, I remembered the debates I had had with people who didn't believe they would ever in their lifetime hear a black man take the presidential oath of office. But I believed. My belief was born out of that movement's goals and achievements, and as I stood on the grounds of the Capitol among the masses of joyful people of all ages and colors, I could not help but think back to the days of marches and demonstrations in unkind places. Back then, protestors took strength from freedom songs, one of which was about how we had come "a mighty long way." I found myself humming that tune.

On the campaign trail in Selma, Alabama, on March 4, 2007, Barack Obama acknowledged his debt to the civil rights movement, saying, "I'm here because somebody marched for our freedom . . . I'm here because all of you sacrificed for me. I stand on the shoulders of giants." He was speaking at the Brown Chapel AME Church, where more than forty years earlier many of the "giants" he spoke of were teenagers and young adults. In that sense, they weren't very different from many of the volunteers I saw during Obama's presidential campaign—handing out leaflets, knocking on doors, and shouting into bullhorns. The young volunteers in 2008 worked with the kind of energy and enthusiasm and desire for change I had not seen since the days of the civil rights movement. The mood, spirit, and activism I saw on college campuses around the country in that winter took me back to the days when young people poured out of their classrooms and into the streets, marching for freedom—freedom to be judged, in Martin Luther King's

Michelle Obama held the Bible for Barack Obama as he took the oath of office.

words, "not by the color of their skin but the content of their character." But there were critical differences, too. While the young volunteers of today may have confronted harsh words, that was as far as it got. The young people of the movement were confronted not only with harsh words, but with harsh deeds—from brutal beatings and torture to imprisonment to murder.

Waiting for the inauguration ceremony to begin, there were times I had to walk away from other people. As I reflected back on the journey that had brought me to that moment, my eyes kept filling with tears that I didn't want to have to explain. Part of my emotion was driven by thoughts of the ones we lost along the way, some from racist violence, others, like my classmate Hamilton Holmes—who walked into history with me through the gates of the University of Georgia—from natural causes. At fifty-four, at the peak of his career as an orthopedic surgeon, Hamp had died suddenly of a heart attack. Vivian Malone, who had desegregated the University of Alabama, had a stroke and died at the age of sixty-three. I kept thinking that had they lived, they would surely have been somewhere in this throng, and I missed their presence.

Dressed for the cold, I waited with the crowd for the inauguration to begin.

But I was also overwhelmed by joy. Back on the campuses I visited in the winter of 2008, when I had finished complimenting the students for their renewed activism, I would ask them to join me in another song that used to keep our feet in the street "until freedom rang," a song that went like this:

Ain't gonna let nobody turn me 'roun'
Turn me 'roun'
Turn me 'roun'
Ain't gonna let nobody turn me 'roun'
Keep on walkin'
Keep on talkin'
Walking up the freedom trail.

I couldn't help thinking what a giant step not just Barack Obama but America was taking this day, walking up the freedom trail.

Barack Obama does indeed stand on the shoulders of giants—thousands of determined men, women, and young people who blazed a trail for him, just as our generation stood on the shoulders of giants who, from the day they were brought to these shores in chains, never accepted the denial of their full humanity, freedom, justice, and rights. How my generation built on that legacy and reached their mountaintops is a remarkable story of faith, perseverance, and courage.

"All the News
That's Fit to Print"

The New Y

CIII...No. 35,178.

Entered as Second-Class Matter.
Post Office. New York. N. Y.

NEW YORK, TUES

IGH COURT BANS SC
-TO-0 DECISION GRA

Carthy Hearing Off a Wee

R IS IRATE

Orders Aides
sclose Details
vel Meeting

etter and excerpts
pt, Pages 24, 25, 26.

. LAWRENCE

he New York Times.

TON, May 17 — A
tive by President
esulted today in an
for at least a week
's Army-McCarthy

and Republican
e publicly and some
dicted that the in-
ight never resume
owever, there were
s who insisted that
on would go on to

Communist Arms Unloaded in Guatemala
By Vessel From Polish Port, U. S. Learns

State Department Views News Gravely Because of Red Infiltration

Special to The New York Times.

WASHINGTON. May 17—The State Department said today that it had reliable information that "an important shipment of arms" had been sent from Communist-controlled territory to Guatemala.

It said the arms, now being unloaded at Puerto Barrios, Guatemala, had been shipped from Stettin, a former German Baltic seaport, which has been occupied by Communist Poland since World War II. The Guatemalan regime has been frequently accused of being influenced by Communists.

"Because of the origin of these arms, the point of their embarka-tion, their destination and the

The New York Times   May 18. 1954
Site of arms arrival (cross)

quantity of arms involved, the Department of State considers that this is a development of gravity." the announcement said.

A freighter arrived at Puerto

Embassy Says Nation of Central America May Buy Munitions Anywhere

Barrios last Saturday, the State Department reported, carrying a large shipment of armament con-signed to the Guatemalan Gov-ernment.

The State Department did not divulge the exact quantity of the arms, their nature or where they had been manufactured.

Reliable sources told The New York Times, however, that ten freight car loads of goods listed in the manifest as "hardware" had been unloaded from this ship and sent to the city of Guatemala since Sunday. Guatemala is 150 miles from Puerto Barrios.

Continued on Page 10. Column 5

rk Times.

k Times Company.

MAY 18, 1954.

Times Square, New York 36, N. Y.
Telephone LAckawanna 4-1000

LATE CITY EDITION

Fair and cool today. Mostly sunny, continued cool tomorrow.
Temperature Range Today-Max., 68; Min., 52
Temperatures Yesterday—Max., 69; Min., 61
Full U. S. Weather Bureau Report, Page 31

FIVE CENT:

HOOL SEGREGATION;
TS TIME TO COMPLY

as Eisenhower Bars Repor

CTION OF SOUTH

thing Spell' for
stment Tempers
gion's Feelings

JOHN N. POPHAM
ecial to The New York Times.
TTANOOGA, Tenn., May
e South's reaction to the
e Court's decision outlaw-
ial segregation in public
appeared to be tempered
rably today.
time lag allowed for car-
t the required transitions
to be the major factor in
action.
ern leaders of both races
ical, educational and com-
servic. fields expressed
t that covered a wide
Some spoke bitter words
rged on defiance. Others
from sharp disagreement

1896 RULING UI

'Separate but E
Doctrine Held Ou
Place in Educati

*Text of Supreme Court de
is printed on Page 1*

By LUTHER A. HUST
Special to The New York Time
WASHINGTON, May 1
Supreme Court unanimous
lawed today racial segrega
public schools.
Chief Justice Earl Warre
two opinions that put the
of unconstitutionality on
systems in twenty-one stat
the District of Columbia
segregation is permissive c
datory.
The court, taking cogniz.
the problems involved in
tegration of the school s

1959

"Our Time Has Come"
—*Atlanta Student Movement slogan*

If I had to select one year in my teenage life that was the most exciting, I would choose 1959, my senior year at Henry McNeal Turner High School in Atlanta, Georgia. It wasn't just the end of an amazing few years—it was also, for me, the start of a historic journey.

Before Turner, my education had been through the second-class schools of a segregated system. I had started elementary school in the small town of Covington, Georgia, where the white administrators who controlled the funds for all schools made certain that black students stayed in a place of inferiority. We often got textbooks from the white schools after they had been used over and over—many were missing pages. We didn't have a cafeteria, but could buy food from a small stand that featured pig ear sandwiches. We could buy bags of fried pork skins to go with them—hardly the kind of nutritious food growing children need. Our

Facing page: George E. C. Hayes, Thurgood Marshall, and James M. Nabrit, the lawyers who led the fight for school integration, posed on the steps of the Supreme Court after segregation was ruled unconstitutional on May 17, 1954.

Previous pages: *The New York Times* front page from May 18, 1954. For full text of school segregation article, see page 145.

playground was just as bad. We had some swings and a rusty merry-go-round, but when it rained, the red Georgia clay turned into red Georgia mud.

Even so, the devotion of our teachers, parents, and the community kept us from feeling inferior. Once a year the school held a fund-raiser to help narrow the gap between the black and white schools. One year, because my mother and grandmother had raised the most money, I was named queen of the school. I got a Bulova watch and a "diamond" tiara, and although I really liked having a real wristwatch, I especially liked being called a queen—one of the many little things black folks did to help keep their children from believing they were as inferior as the white folks tried to make them out to be.

In 1954, the United States Supreme Court ruled that "separate but equal"—the idea that segregation was acceptable as long as the same facilities were provided for both whites and blacks—violated the Fourteenth Amendment of the United States Constitution guaranteeing equal protection of the law. But even though the highest court in the land had ruled against racial segregation, no states in the Deep South moved to desegregate. In fact, white officials in Georgia passed laws that would set up private white schools rather than desegregate. "Separate and unequal" continued in schools, trains, and buses, and in public spaces like parks, lunch counters, and bathrooms. Whites ran everything that mattered—from the economy to voter registration.

By that time, my family had moved to the big city of Atlanta and I was in the seventh grade at a previously all-white elementary school (the whites had moved out as soon as the first black family moved into the area known as Mozley Park). But the historic ruling was not even discussed in my classroom or in the school, so fearful were black teachers of the white-run school system. The state had decreed that any teacher affiliated with the National Association for the Advancement of Colored People (NAACP)—the civil rights organization that had been victorious in challenging school segregation—would be barred from ever teaching in the state.

When I graduated from elementary school, I enrolled at Turner High School. In many ways, it was an idyllic island in a sea of segregation. The black teachers at Turner also made it a part of their mission to protect us from the negative psychological effects of segregation. Although they couldn't give us first-class citizenship, they gave us a first-class sense of ourselves.

Even though Atlanta was as segregated as any place in the South, with its "whites only" bathrooms, water fountains, and lunch counters, Black Atlanta was in some respects much better off than rural areas in Georgia and other cities and towns throughout the South. Black Atlanta reveled in being the home of the Atlanta University Complex—made up of some of the finest black colleges in the country. The city had a solid middle class, with prosperous black businesses. We lived happily apart and generally removed from the worst manifestations of segregation, hardly ever encountering overt hostility from whites.

And yet, there was always something to remind us that once we ventured outside our communities, we had to make allowances for the culture we had no control over. Because the department stores where we shopped did not serve blacks in their restaurants, we always ate before we left home. And although our families had charge accounts at the major downtown department stores, we usually went to shop only when we needed to buy shoes or dresses for a special occasion, like Easter or the first day of school. The salespeople were not impolite, but there clearly was a difference between the way they treated blacks and the way they related to whites.

Once, my mother and I were shopping together. Her skin was so fair she looked white. Although we were standing side by side at the counter looking at some scarves, we were not talking to each other when the saleswoman came up. Ignoring me into invisibility, she smiled at my mother and asked quite nicely what she could do for her. When my mother said, "You have to ask my daughter; she's the one we're shopping for," the woman looked from my mother to me and her entire demeanor changed. She became abrupt and less polite. "Oh," she said, with near-derision, "I didn't see *her*."

There were other examples of the price paid by blacks for the lie of "separate but equal." In order to go to the Fox, the main movie theater in Atlanta, black people had to climb several flights of stairs on the outside of the building, which was built like a castle. At the top was the "crow's nest," where blacks had to sit.

Despite a Supreme Court ruling requiring integration, public facilities, schools, waiting rooms, eating establishments, and movie theaters such as this one in Mississippi (photographed in 1939) were still segregated in 1961.

And then there were the trips my mother, grandmother, and I took to visit my cousins in rural Social Circle, Georgia. My mother always made sure we had plenty of brown paper bags in case one of us had to go to the bathroom. We could fill the car at gas stations, but not use the restrooms. Once, when I had to go really badly, my mother pulled off the road near some tall weeds. I ventured a small distance into the weeds and squatted. When I got back into the car, I felt stings on my legs. It seemed as if every time I scratched, the stinging would break out farther up my leg. My mother turned on the interior car lights to reveal my scrawny little legs covered with ants.

Such was the legacy of a country that defined blacks in 1787 as "three-fifths of a person." That inclusion in the Constitution was a concession to white Southerners who didn't want to recognize their slaves as full human beings, but needed to have them counted to give the Southern whites a greater share of seats in the House of Representatives. That would enable the Southern whites to protect their interests, including slavery. The North thought it unfair to count the slaves, since they were not free, but in the end, North and South agreed to the three-fifths compromise. While Southern whites rejoiced at their victory, blacks suffered under a law that defined each of them as less than a person. The 1857 *Dred Scott* decision upheld the idea that a black man only constituted three-fifths of a person and declared, "any person descended from Africans is not a citizen."

The Emancipation Proclamation eventually freed Southern slaves in 1863, and a series of constitutional amendments—the thirteenth, fourteenth, and fifteenth—which were passed over the next seven years, were designed to erase the reality of a country "half slave and half free," in the words of Abraham Lincoln. For a brief period following the Civil War, Southern blacks were allowed to vote and run for office. But this freedom was short-lived. The *Dred Scott* decision was upheld in 1896 in the case of *Plessy v. Ferguson,* in which Homer Plessy was arrested, tried, and convicted for sitting in the section designated for whites on an East Louisiana Railroad train. As a result, a wave of new state constitutions and laws entrenching white privilege followed. Named "Jim Crow," for a song initially sung by a white actor in black face, these rules limiting freedoms for the black population became the law and would remain so for decades.

During that time, blacks were oppressed and brutalized in some of the most sadistic ways. They were hanged from trees and tortured before dying—burned, dismembered, or sometimes dragged behind cars before they died. Between

1889 and 1930, an estimated 3,700 black men and women were lynched, although the figure may have been higher, because many lynchings went unreported.

I will never forget a 1955 issue of *Jet* magazine, a publication owned by and published for and about blacks. It featured an image so horrifying it was hard to

look at. Emmett Till had gone from his home in Chicago to the small town of Money, Mississippi, to visit relatives. Being a boy of fourteen and not knowing the Jim Crow codes of the segregated South, young Till whistled at a white woman in a grocery store shortly after he got there. Three days later, he was abducted from his bed by two white men. They beat him severely, gouged out one eye, then shot him in the head, tied him with barbed wire to a cotton gin, and threw him

In September 1955, Emmett Till's mother, Mamie Bradley, and a relative attended the Mississippi trial of the men who murdered her son. The accused were acquitted, though they later admitted their guilt.

into the Tallahatchee River. His mangled, bloated body was pulled from the river three days later.

Even though there were bombings of the homes of some blacks in Atlanta who moved into previously all-white neighborhoods, our life at Turner High School was far removed from the violence. And even though we learned about Dred Scott and *Plessy*, we also studied a different history, rarely included in textbooks at the time. We learned about women like Harriet Tubman, a former slave who helped slaves escape to the North via a route that came to be known as "the Underground Railroad." We also learned about successful, pioneering black women like educator Mary McLeod Bethune, poet Phyllis Wheatley, and crusading journalist Ida B. Wells. And we learned about the "race men" who fought against the images of blacks perpetuated in white culture as clowning, singing, and dancing fools. They preached dignity and sought justice and equality for blacks. Our teachers made sure we learned those lessons, whether or not they consciously believed they were giving us the tools to tear down the system.

By 1959, some of the more courageous blacks in Atlanta had grown weary of waiting for the *Brown* decision against segregation to become a living reality. There had been attempts at desegregation at the college level, but few had been successful. A group of young black professionals called the Atlanta Committee for Cooperative Action (ACCA) had begun to think about how to move faster on opening up the lily-white system of public higher education, believing that would pry open doors in other areas of the segregated system.

Sometime during my busy senior year, two black men from ACCA, Carl Holman and Jesse Hill, arrived at Turner High School. They were looking for a couple of students with good educational and moral credentials to apply to one of the local white colleges as a test of the *Brown* decision. The idea was for a highly qualified black student to submit an application to enroll in one of the traditionally white state schools. When the application was inevitably rejected, ACCA could use that rejection as the basis for a legal case that could force the state to desegregate.

In their earlier deliberations about candidates, ACCA had ruled out high schoolers and had attempted to enroll an older student. She was denied on the basis of having a child out of wedlock. The decision was totally unfair, but ACCA felt that it was a losing battle. So they came looking for two students who didn't have any issues that could be challenged. The first two students our principal Daniel Davis thought of were Hamilton "Hamp" Holmes, who was co-captain of the football team and first in our class of over 150, and me. I was third in the class; in my second year as editor of the *Green Light*, the school newspaper; president of the Honor Society; and winner of the hotly contested position of homecoming queen.

I wasn't concerned that day when we were summoned to the principal's office—as class leaders, it wasn't unusual for the principal to want to have a word with us. When we got to his office, we were introduced to the two men, and without much beating around the bush, they asked if we would be interested in attending one of the Atlanta-based colleges in the state university system, which we knew was all-white.

We had both been accepted at other schools, but this was tempting. The school where I had been accepted to study journalism was far from home, in Detroit, Michigan. In those days, segregated states would pay blacks "out of state aid" as an enticement to leave to study elsewhere if they wanted to pursue graduate or professional courses only offered at white schools. For his part, Hamp was proud of the history of the all-male Morehouse College, where he had been accepted. But here were some of the pillars of the black community. They also regarded Morehouse highly, but they were committed to a different purpose.

Hamp and I both came from race-conscious families. Hamp's grandfather and father had been pioneers in the fifties when they led the fight to desegregate Atlanta's golf courses. My father was a chaplain in the army and had championed the rights of black soldiers when the army was still segregated during the 1940s and early 1950s. We didn't know much about the white schools in Atlanta, but without much deliberation, we told the men we would be interested. I don't think at the time we had any idea what it would entail, but we felt a sense of responsibility to give it a try.

When we visited Georgia State College a few weeks later, Hamp and I surprised the adults who had taken us there. After looking at the course offerings, we told them we didn't think the institution offered us what we wanted. And then Hamilton surprised everybody, including me. As we were leaving, in his usual deliberate way of speaking, he said, "I think I would like to try over there," and pointed north. I knew immediately what he meant before he said it. "The university," he quickly added. "That's where I want to go." And I agreed.

Georgia State College didn't have the kind of facilities the University of Georgia had to help Hamp achieve his dream of becoming a doctor. And the only journalism school in the state was at the University of Georgia. But it had been all-white since it opened its doors in 1785, the oldest public university in the United States.

For the next few months, Hamp and I were busy getting our applications ready to submit to the university. The local NAACP helped with the payments associated with the process because they anticipated we would probably end up in court and would need good documentation of our efforts. At the same time, members of ACCA began patrolling in front of my house because they were concerned about the possibility of bombings. And since my father was away on military duty, there were no adult men in the house.

My yearbook photo as "most popular senior."

On July 11, 1959, a story about our application appeared in the *Atlanta Constitution,* a white-owned and -run newspaper. The university's registrar was quoted saying the university was already full and that they were turning down would-be freshmen, except for bona fide residents of Athens, the town where the university was located.

Finally, we got a letter turning us down on those grounds. It was a clever way of avoiding being challenged on the basis of race, which they knew they could not defend after the *Brown* decision. In my case, they also declared that there was no room in the dorms and Georgia required female students to live on campus. Until we could force a legal decision to allow us to attend the university, Hamp and I would continue with our original plans for school. In the fall, I went to Wayne State University in Detroit, and Hamp went to Morehouse. We were still wending our way through administrative and legal steps when a new day dawned and effectively gave birth to the civil rights movement—the Greensboro, North Carolina, sit-ins.

OF THEM VEXED

Is on Need to Counter shchev Proposal for al World Disarming

NA ADAMS SCHMIDT
cial to The New York Times.

HINGTON, Feb. 14— States officials expressed today that they would systematic disarmament dy in time to submit to stern disarmament dele- heads now meeting here. of the delegates repre- Britain, France, Italy nada are expressing irri- tnat they should have l so far to find the leader Western alliance unpre- or the task of working Western counter to Pre- hrushchev's call for total lisarmament.

ive Western delegations et delegates of five So- c nations — the Soviet Poland, Czechoslovakia, y and Rumania—in Ge- thirty days.

to Soviet Intentions

t from the propaganda nce of answering the proposal, diplomats here the Geneva meeting will pportunities to probe for intentions at the East- ummit meeting in the

diplomats maintain that ier Khrushchev is seri- ut "coexistence," and if ously would like to de- ore Soviet wealth to im- living standards at - as many Britons and Americans believe—then be expected to prepare Geneva meeting for a sig- decision on disarma- t the summit.

ng the disarmament gathered here the view espread that France's omic explosion yesterday

---

WASHINGTON, Feb. 14— The long-awaited civil rights debate will get under way in the Senate tomorrow.

A struggle of weeks and per- haps months lies ahead, with the Southerners using every tactic in opposition. On the other hand, Northern Democrats and Republicans face the problem of bridging their differences and agreeing on a common ap- proach.

On the eve of the debate it became known that Senator Thomas C. Hennings Jr., Mis- souri Democrat, had drafted a new proposal to protect Ne- groes' voting rights. His idea is to combine features of the two plans previously advanced, one by the Civil Rights Com- mission and one by the Justice Department.

The commission called for the President to name registrars,

The New York Times

Thomas C. Hennings Jr.

on the recommendation of the commission, to qualify Negroes to vote in Federal elections. The Justice Department, backed by President Eisenhower, pro-

Continued on Page 19, Column 1

Negro Sitdowns Stir Fear Of Wider Unrest in South

By CLAUDE SITTON
Special to The New York Times.

CHARLOTTE, N. C., Feb. 14—Negro student demon- strations against segregated eating facilities have raised grave questions in the South over the future of the region's race relations. A sounding of opinion in the affected areas showed that much more might be involved than the matter of the Negro's right to sit at a lunch counter for a coffee break.

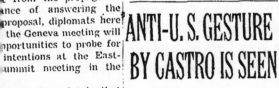

ANTI-U.S. GESTURE BY CASTRO IS SEEN

Moscow Deal Said to Show Stress on Independence —Red Influence Noted

By JAMES RESTON
Special to The New York Times.

HAVANA, Feb. 14—The Cuban Government is conscious- ly moving closer to the Soviet Union to demonstrate its in- dependence of the United States.

This seems to be the opinion

The demonstrations were gen- erally dismissed at first as an- other college fad of the "panty- raid" variety. This opinion lost adherents, however, as the movement spread from North Carolina to Virginia, Florida, South Carolina and Tennessee and involved fifteen cities.

Some whites wrote off the episodes as the work of "out- side agitators." But even they conceded that the seeds of dis- sent had fallen in fertile soil.

Backed by Negro Leaders

Appeals from white leaders

Plants by La e 190

By JOHN W. FINNE
Special to The New York Times
WASHINGTON, Feb. 14 Atomic Energy Commissio offer a ten-year reactor gram to Congress this we is designed to achieve eco nuclear electricity by th Nineteen Sixties in areas United States that have cost power.

The plan will be presen the Joint Congressional mittee on Atomic Energy begins its annual hearings day on the status of the a program.

From a political, technic psychological standpoint hearings should mark a t point in the atomic powe gram, which in the pas been notable more for po bickering and technical se than progress toward ge ing electricity.

Long Urged by Congr

A long-range plan for opment and constructic nuclear power reactors is that has long been deman the Congressional committ until recently has been r by the commission.

The reactor progran which the Government ha spending over $100,000, year for several years, undergo a fundamental re under the ten-year plan stead of the past approa pursuing every promising tor concept, the commissic propose concentrating on ited number that seem t the most promise of pro economic electricity in th future.

Also implicit in the p a shift away from the philosophy—much criticiz Democrats on the Congre committee—of relying pri on private industry to car load of building developn atomic power plants.

Will Develop Prototy

The commission, in effe assume a responsibility t atomic reactors up throu

on Share of B

ext of statement by Moore is printed on Page 20.

By PETER KIHSS

rank C. Moore expressed
azement yesterday that City
ntroller Lawrence E. Gerosa
d joined in a statement with
ayor Wagner Saturday at-
king fiscal proposals for the
y.

r. Moore is acting chair-
n of a state commission that
de the proposals while in-
tigating the city's affairs.

nable to reach Mr. Gerosa
ing the day, Mr. Moore an-
nced that he was calling off
meeting he had scheduled
today with the Controller.

declared that Mr. Gerosa
mised last Thursday that
re would be no statement
the Controller or his staff
or to today's meeting.

n this basis, Mr. Moore said
t he could not believe that
Controller had joined with
Mayor in Saturday's twen-
page, point-by-point attack
the commission's Feb. 1 re-
t. The attack described the
ort as "replete with contra-
ions, exaggerations and in-
sistencies" and "pie-in-the-
" financial proposals.

overnor, Backs Commission

leanwhile Governor Rocke-
er asserted in a telecast that
commission had made
nd" proposals that "would
the city on the way back to
pay-as-you-go basis." The
ernor charged that the
gner-Gerosa statement con-
ed generalities that were
fusing and misleading to
public."

tto L. Nelson Jr., who reed as chairman of the nine-
her commission last Tues-
defended the fiscal pro-
ls as "true and valid." He
ted each point would mean
rtant savings, contrary to
Wagner-Gerosa statement.
Nelson also voiced hope
the report would help bring
t charter reform here.

A Threefold Plan

The New York Times

ASSAILS CITY POLITICIANS: Governor Rockefeller on the Citizens Union "Searchlight" yesterday.

City's General Income Put At Record $781,168,000

By PAUL CROWELL

Controller Lawrence E. Gerosa estimated at a record
$781,168,000 yesterday the city's general fund revenues for
the fiscal year starting next July 1. In a report to the
Board of Estimate and the
City Council, Mr. Gerosa predicted that the total would
consist of $738,576,000 of
actual receipts and a $42,-
592,000 cash carry-over on
June 30 from the general fund
for 1959-60.

The $42,595,000 carry-over
item is not a surplus, however,
in the sense that it can be put
to any use the city desires. It
must be carried over into the
general fund of the succeeding
fiscal year. Its effect is to
help reduce real estate taxes
in the next fiscal year.

Source of General Fund

The city's general fund receipts are derived from taxes
other than those on real estate,
from fees, licenses, permits,
rents and similar charges, and

REVISION IS URGED IN YOUTH DRIVING

Albany Bill Would Require Training of 16-Year-Olds for a License at 17

By WARREN WEAVER Jr.
Special to The New York Times.

ALBANY, Feb. 14—A state-
wide plan to teach all teen-agers
how to drive will be submitted
to the Legislature tomorrow.

It envisions making driver
education available to every
student in every public or pri-

City's Delegation a
Switched Position
a Phone Call, He

By CLAYTON KN(

Governor Rockefelle
day bluntly put the b
the rupture of frien
state relationships o
Wagner and city repres
in the Legislature.

He accused the May
representation, tinged
dacity," in saying t
fiscal needs had been i
the state budget. In
asserted, city deman
submitted "two days
budget had gone to pr

Hinting broadly at
trol, the Governor s
agreements he had rea
the Mayor somehow
been "translated into
support of these prog
the city's legislative re
tives and those who
[these] legislators."

Last-Minute Shift

"I don't know who
them," he said. "But a
is that they can make
and take positions u
time of the vote and
whole group can go t
direction."

He cited how "a ph
from New York City"
duced Democrats to vot
a program to aid c
railroads that they ha
prepare and had been
ing. He said that ever
crat had voted agai
year's increase in the
tax, which W. Averell
man, his Democratic
cessor as Governor, had

"If anyone is short
the city for political pu
Mr. Rockefeller said,
city's own representat
Albany who are playi
tics with this thing."

1960

"Ain't Gonna Let Nobody Turn Me 'Roun' . . ."

—*African American spiritual*

It all started out like any other college bull session. In one of their rooms, four black students at North Carolina Agricultural and Technical College got together "to discuss current events, political events, things that affected us—pretty much as college kids do today," remembered Joe McNeil, one of the four. They were typical college students, but as the night went on, the college bull session turned into a historic conversation, one that would launch the civil rights movement. Sometime during the night, the four decided to stage a sit-in at Woolworth's five-and-dime, a place where blacks shopped and could buy a soda at the lunch counter, but weren't allowed to sit—they had to stand up and drink it.

This was true all over the South, so when McNeil, Junior Blair, Frank McCain, and David Richmond sat down at the lunch counter about 4:30 in the afternoon of February 1, 1960, "people started to look at us," McNeil recalled. "The help, many of whom were black, looked at us in disbelief, too. They were

Facing page: A member of the Congress of Racial Equality's school of nonviolence demonstrated how to protect vital parts of the body if attacked.

Previous pages: *The New York Times* front page from February 15, 1960. For full text of sit-in article, see page 149.

Joseph McNeil, Franklin McCain, William Smith, and Clarence Henderson sat in at the Greensboro Woolworth lunch counter on February 2, 1960, the second day of the protest.

concerned about our safety. We asked for service and we were denied, and we expected to be denied. We asked why couldn't we be served, and obviously we weren't given a reasonable answer, and it was our intent to sit there until they decided to serve us."

In fact, anticipating they wouldn't be served at the lunch counter, they had earlier bought items like toothpaste and toothbrushes from the store so that when the white waitress told them they couldn't be served, their ironic reply was that they already had been. McCain recalled years later that at the time, he "felt invincible fifteen seconds after I sat on that stool and, quite honestly, I wouldn't have felt cheated if I had died at that moment because I had gone to my moun-taintop and I saw the other side."

After a few hours, the four left, planning to return the following day, which they did, and the day after that—only, as the word got around among the other college students, more and more protestors joined them. By week's end, they were joined by more than a thousand students, including three white students from nearby Greensboro Women's College. No violence occurred, but the threat of it hung heavily in the air, and even thirty-three years later, Gloria Brown Wise, one of the first of many women to sit in, could still remember her anxiety at the time. "I was scared," Wise, who was twenty-one when the sit-in occurred, re-called. "We knew what could happen to us. We knew it was a time when we were being watched very carefully." In the coming days, her fear was justified. The students were viciously attacked, one with scalding coffee, another with a lit cigarette, while the police stood by, ominously slapping their hands with their billy clubs.

Still, the protestors persevered. In small groups, they would calmly walk into segregated restaurants and take seats at the lunch counter as if nothing was out of the ordinary, making a peaceful statement opposing the "whites only" policy that kept them from getting service. By July 25, after the sit-ins had cost them some $200,000 in lost income, Woolworth's desegregated all of its lunch counters, and the civil rights movement had its first victory.

The idea behind the Greensboro sit-ins quickly spread to other campuses and other cities in North and South Carolina. On February 13, it reached Nashville, Tennessee, where students had been preparing for their turn. They had attended workshops that taught nonviolence—their teachers, like divinity student James Lawson, believed that "the most practical reason [for the sit-ins] is that we're try-ing to create a more just society. You cannot do it if you exaggerate the ani-mosities." So the young students were grounded in the nonviolent teachings of Mahatma Gandhi, the Indian spiritual leader who used nonviolence to help India achieve its independence from Britain in 1947. Nonviolent protestors were taught not to hit back, but to protect themselves against the brutality that was likely to come.

"We would practice things such as how to protect your head from a beating and how to protect each other," recalled Diane Nash. A Chicago native, she had come south to attend Fisk University. Although she came from a Northern city with some racial problems of its own, she was still stunned at the extent of racism in Tennessee. Diane became one of the leaders of the Nashville Movement.

"If one person was taking a severe beating," she recalled, "we would practice other people putting their bodies in between that person and the violence, so that the violence could be more distributed and hopefully no one would get seriously injured. We would practice not striking back if someone struck us."

And those tactics came in handy, for as the Nashville sit-ins progressed, so did the danger. On one occasion, a group of white men attacked the students, especially the women, "putting lighted cigarettes down their backs, in their hair," a protestor named John Lewis later recalled.

The protestors were arrested.

"To go to jail was to bring shame and disgrace on the family," Lewis said. It went against everything these young black students had been taught at home. But they hoped the arrests would get national publicity that would embarrass the federal government into either helping or protecting them.

Lewis and others came to see being jailed as part of what he called "a holy crusade." And, as Diane Nash recalled, "The movement had a way of reaching inside you and bringing out things that even you didn't know were there. Such as courage. When it was time to go to jail, I was much too busy to be afraid." As she saw it, they "started feeling the power of the idea whose time had come."

In April of that year, a woman named Ella Baker called a meeting of 120 student leaders at Shaw University in Raleigh, North Carolina. Baker was the executive director of the three-year-old Southern Christian Leadership Conference (SCLC), an organization of mostly young Christian preachers led by Martin Luther King, Jr. By this time, some 50,000 black students and white sympathizers had been involved in the rapidly growing sit-in movement. Baker served as a role model and mentor, gently guiding the students without attempting to take over. It was her speech at the conference, "More than a Hamburger," that helped young activists like Julian Bond, from the newborn Atlanta Movement, to understand that "racial problems extended far beyond lunch counters."

The meeting eventually concluded with the students forming a civil rights organization to represent the younger, more impatient, generation—the Student Nonviolent Coordinating Committee—also known as SNCC (pronounced "snick").

For the first time, students as young as seventeen and eighteen were organized into a powerful force bent on changing a system that had been in effect since before their parents, grandparents, and even great-grandparents were born. From that point on, SNCC contributed the "shock troops" of the movement, venturing to the danger zones throughout the South where most everyone else feared to tread.

SNCC had a new approach to the local people where they set up shop. They worked from the grass roots, the bottom up, rather than dictating from the top down. That meant working to empower the local people to achieve their rights. SNCC taught reading and writing and citizenship to rural blacks, helping them meet unfair literacy requirements that prevented many from voting, and its members demonstrated the kind of courage that would almost always be needed to challenge often-violent white authority.

Eventually other organizations came to work alongside SNCC, including the SCLC, the Congress of Racial Equality (CORE), and even the National Association for the Advancement of Colored People (NAACP). Founded in 1909, the NAACP had long been quietly agitating for civil rights. Although the organization worked on many battlefronts, including lobbying Congress and building branches to fight discrimination locally, its primary battlefield was the courts. The legal avenue was long and arduous and gained little publicity. But it was the efforts of the NAACP that had won the *Brown* decision in 1954, laying the groundwork for the younger generation's activism. And while the younger activists had little patience with the legal route to equality, when SNCC members or those from any other organization engaged in direct-action protests like sit-ins, it was often the legal team from the NAACP and its Legal Defense Fund—known as the Inc Fund—that bailed them out of jail.

While the sit-in movement spread to more than 100 cities in 1960, the Nashville Movement was probably the most successful and best organized. Young demonstrators marched on City Hall and there, Diane Nash challenged Mayor Ben West, "as a man, as a person." She stood face-to-face, talking directly to him as he had probably never been spoken to by a black person, and as a result, Nash got him to concede for the first time in his life that in his heart he knew it was wrong for black citizens of Nashville to be denied seats at the lunch counters on the basis of race.

Being so far away in Detroit, I watched these events with admiration and some frustration. I knew that even if I were there, where it was all happening, I would have to stick to my own battle and not jeopardize my chances of eventually getting into the University of Georgia. Still, it was hard to watch from the sidelines, and it got harder when I came home for breaks and found my old classmates, who were now at one or another of the black colleges within the Atlanta University System, preparing to sit in and challenge the lie of "separate but equal" in Atlanta. But if I were to participate and be arrested, it would give the university a "legitimate" reason to reject my application.

Martin Luther King, Jr., (center) met with a group of student sit-in organizers, including Julian Bond (in white shirt) during a strategy meeting in his office, September, 1960.

Julian Bond, son of a distinguished black educator, Horace Mann Bond, and one of the founders of SNCC, was one of the leaders of the Atlanta Student Movement, along with leaders from the all-black local colleges, including Lonnie King from Morehouse and Ruby Doris Smith and Herschelle Challenor from Spelman.

I didn't get to know them as well as I got to know Julian during that time. He was tall, with a baby face, and soft-spoken. And he was totally dedicated to the movement. But he also enjoyed the parties the students frequently gave to help relieve some of the tension built up in the demonstrations and arrests. Although Julian was not the best dancer in the crowd, he applied his subtle wit to the poetry he liked to write, at least one inspired by those parties. It went:

> *See that girl*
> *shake that thing.*
> *We can't all be*
> *Martin Luther King.*

I got most of my information on the movement from my two best friends from high school, Carolyn and Wilma Long. By this time, they were students at Atlanta's all-black Clark College, one of the five institutions that made up the Atlanta University System.

In the fall of 1960, Atlanta students from all the colleges in that system hit the streets, 4,000 strong. Some of them had met with the Greensboro Students Movement, and they and the Atlanta students had their methods. But they tailored them to fit what they saw as "the historical legacy of Black Atlanta."

"So we approached the problem very scientifically," Carolyn Long told me. "We studied it, went downtown, and actually counted the numbers of seats at lunch counters. We came up with solutions, and we mapped out strategies."

They also were taught tactics for survival in the near certainty they would be attacked: "They taught us how to crouch and cover our heads in case we were being clubbed by police," Carolyn said, ". . . also to fall down and pull our knees up over our stomachs in a fetal position, so the brunt of the blows would be on the meat of our bodies, like the back and the behind."

The organizers also ruled out participation by high school students, whom they believed were too young to be exposed to the inevitable harassment and possible brutality and jailing.

The Atlanta students pored over studies done earlier on patterns of segregation and enlisted students in the English departments at the various colleges to help draft a document reflecting those problems. Then Julian, Lonnie King, and several other students, calling themselves The Committee on Appeal for Human Rights, fashioned it into "An Appeal for Human Rights." It was signed by the student body presidents of the six affiliated institutions forming the Atlanta University Center: Clark, Morehouse, Morris Brown, and Spelman Colleges; Atlanta University; and the Interdenominational Theological Center. On March 9, 1960, they published a full-page ad in all the Atlanta newspapers. It stated:

> Today's youth will not sit by submissively while being denied all the rights and privileges and joys of life . . . We do not intend to wait placidly for those rights which are legally and morally ours to be meted out to us one at a time.

The black newspaper the *Atlanta Daily World* refused to publish it, worried that they might lose their white advertisers.

The Appeal spelled out the students' rationale for demanding an end to segregation, stating that it was "not in keeping with the ideals of Democracy and Christianity." And it went on to talk about the impact of segregation—"robbing not only the segregated but the segregator of his human dignity."

The well-researched document pointed out that a black man "paid his fair share of taxes, but does not enjoy participation in city, county, and state government at the level where laws are enacted" and it went on to point out that churches "foster segregation of the races to the point of making Sunday the most segregated day of the week."

The document ended by calling on all people of authority to "abolish these injustices" and vowing to "use every legal and non-violent means at our disposal to secure full citizenship rights of this great Democracy of ours."

That day, Carolyn recalled, some 4,000 students took to the streets of downtown Atlanta. Because of the code of conduct their parents had instilled in them, they were always extremely careful about how they presented themselves in public, so many, like Carolyn, dressed up in their Sunday best and fancy shoes, which in those days were likely to have spike heels. And they marched through the streets chanting, "Our time has come."

This generation was very different from their parents, who loathed segregation but often were afraid to challenge it. Although our parents had shielded us as best they could from the worst manifestations of segregation, they had also given us the tools that enabled us to begin taking control of our destiny. Now we were taking the lessons they had taught us about our past—the slavery, the segregation, and the denial of our basic civil and human rights—and folding them into a new era of struggle against those deprivations. And although we had been privileged children of a proud black community, and were taught to be respectful of our elders, we didn't mind confronting even those black adults who stood against us. We all embraced the watchwords of the Atlanta Student Movement: "Ain't gonna let nobody turn me 'roun'."

When there was no response to their appeal, the students staged the first of many sit-ins aimed at challenging the Jim Crow laws.

By May, as the schools closed for the summer break, the students suspended their protests and most went home. But not all.

Among the exciting activities of that summer was the creation of the *Atlanta Inquirer*. It was born on July 31 out of a need to give a voice to those who were all but banished from the *Atlanta Daily World*. M. Carl Holman, an English professor at Clark College and one of the men who had recruited Hamp and me, was editor of the new paper.

In the *Inquirer,* I saw an opportunity to make a contribution to the struggle that wouldn't put my application to UGA at risk. The paper allowed me to really lend support to the movement, while learning more about journalism. Although the sit-ins had been put on hold, segregation hadn't. So there was always something to cover in black Atlanta. It was often the case that the students were arrested in the morning, bailed out in the afternoon, and came to the professor's basement afterward to share their experiences so we could write them up and put

Martin Luther King, Jr., arrested for assisting an Atlanta student sit-in, was escorted in handcuffs to a hearing on violation of his probation in October 1960.

them in the paper. Julian Bond was also on the staff, eventually becoming managing editor.

I RETURNED TO WAYNE at the end of the summer of 1960 and watched from afar as demonstrations resumed. The students returned to the Atlanta university campuses and began protest planning anew. On October 19, Carolyn and Wilma were among the students who put their feet in the streets and to the fire, joining a demonstration that would have the most far-reaching consequences of any in Atlanta so far. Among their targets was the Magnolia lunchroom at Rich's, the largest department store in Atlanta. For the first time, Martin Luther King, Jr., had been persuaded by the students to join their protest. By now, the movement had a new approach and mantra—"jail without bail," which they hoped would not only fill the jails but would force the Jim Crow laws to be challenged in court. Around fifty protestors were arrested, including Carolyn and Wilma, as well as Dr. King. If convicted, they could have faced ninety-nine years in prison.

The men and women were separated, and the women got the worst of it. Carolyn remembered: "We were placed in a big open cell with murderers, prostitutes, hardened criminals. There were not enough beds, and what beds there were were cold steel slabs. It was cold, so we slept in our clothes. We had dressed up for the demonstrations [as did all students, starting in Nashville] so at first the only shoes we had on were the high heels we wore when we were arrested. So we walked around barefoot on that cold tile floor."

Carolyn, the older of the two sisters, was stoic. Wilma cried. Still, the protestors stuck to their commitment—jail without bail, and some 2,000 students back at the colleges poured into the streets in support, closing sixteen more lunch counters.

By Saturday, the Committee on Appeal for Human Rights expanded the boycott beyond lunch counters, declaring a new goal to "bankrupt the economy of segregation." They carried picket signs reading "Wear old clothes for dignity." As the Ku Klux Klan staged counter demonstrations, black adults, fearful for their children, reached a compromise with the white city fathers, as we called the white officials. The students would be released from jail, but would not demonstrate for

When the students' Committee on Appeal for Human Rights in Atlanta extended their boycott beyond the lunch counters in November 1960, the Ku Klux Klan retaliated by handing out leaflets to shoppers at Rich's department store.

thirty days while they worked out a settlement with the white business community. All of the students were persuaded by this development to leave, except Carolyn, who suspected something was up and who insisted Dr. King tell her personally that he was also leaving. Finally, the jailers brought Dr. King to her, and he persuaded her he was leaving, too. He then took her by the hand and led her to the door, where quite suddenly he pushed her out before he slammed it shut with him inside. Dr. King was held on an earlier, minor traffic infraction—failing to replace his Alabama license with one from Georgia. He would be sentenced to four months of hard labor, a punishment that was reduced when presidential candidate John F. Kennedy called Mrs. King and had his brother, Robert F. Kennedy, lean on the judge.

The agreement with what the students called "the white power structure" didn't last and the students took to the streets again. They handed out up to 70,000 leaflets at churches to educate the black community and expand their support among the reluctant adults. Over in New Orleans, six-year-old Ruby

Bridges was undergoing the same trials as the Little Rock Nine had three years earlier. Once again, vicious threats led President Eisenhower to send in federal marshalls to escort her past leering whites as she became the first black student to attend William Frantz elementary school. But segregation and white resistance continued. No white students attended class with her, and only one white teacher would teach her. Agitated white parents threatened to poison her, and her family also paid a price—her father was fired from his job and her sharecropper grandparents were driven from the fields where they had worked.

Through the fall, I watched these events unfold from afar. But in December, I was summoned to come home for the trial that would pit Hamilton and me against the state of Georgia.

The trial lasted a week, during which we thought Constance Baker Motley of the NAACP Legal Defense Fund and Donald Hollowell, a local cooperating attorney, scored big points with their evidence of the university's duplicity and deception. Vernon Jordan, a young, newly minted lawyer working for Mr. Hollowell, had scoured hundreds of applications at the university and found the application of a white student who had exactly the same elements and timeline as mine. The university hadn't told *her* there was no room in the dormitories; she had been admitted. The judge, William Bootle, sat stolid and stone faced throughout, so there was no way of reading what he was thinking.

After the Christmas holidays, I returned to Wayne State, ready to begin another semester. But on January 6, 1961, I had just gotten back into my room in Detroit when Katherine Johnson, a reporter for the Associated Press, called asking for my reaction to the judge's ruling. She had gotten to me before my mother or my lawyers had a chance to call and tell me that Judge Bootle had ordered Hamilton and me enrolled immediately for classes at the University of Georgia.

Some of my Northern classmates, whose only knowledge of the South was of the vicious violence of white segregationists they had seen on television, started to cry. But I told them not to worry. My time had come. They helped me pack my trunk as I hurriedly prepared to leave for home and the most challenging, but rewarding experience of my life thus far. I was nineteen years old.

By A. H. RASKIN

Sympathy tie-ups by truck-drivers and railroad freight handlers yesterday deepened the impact of the day-old strike on New York's railroad ferry-boats and other harbor craft. The new moves threatened to paralyze most of the city's freight operations.

Federal peacemakers called a night conference of union and management negotiators in an effort to end the stoppage before it caused major hardship. They were spurred by a fear that unionized longshoremen would further immobilize the port by joining teamsters and freight handlers in respecting the strikers' picket lines.

The meeting was recessed at 11:50 P. M. with no apparent progress. Talks will resume at 11 o'clock this morning.

The immediate effect of the walkout of 660 marine employes of eleven railroads was to com-pel 30,000 New Jersey commuters to scramble for substitute transportation to Manhattan.

As a result, there was heavy crowding on buses and trains of the Pennsylvania and Hudson and Manhattan (Hudson Tubes) Railroads. Tunnels and bridges also were jammed as suburban-ites organized car pools to get from one side of the Hudson to the other.

An embargo on rail freight for Manhattan, Brooklyn and the Bronx cut off delivery of thousands of carloads of food, fuel oil and other commodities.

The Teamsters Joint Council, representing all the city's truck drivers, voted unanimously last night to honor all picket lines established by the striking rail crews. John J. O'Rourke, president of the council, said formal instructions would go out today

Continued on Page 22, Column 4

GRAFT IS CHARGED IN BUILDING UNIT

State Investigators Assail 'Virtually Every Stage' of City Plan Examining

By EDITH EVANS ASBURY

The state Commission of Investigation charged yesterday that corruption exists "at virtually every stage" of operations in the plan-examining division of the city Buildings Department.

The accusation is made in a forty-two-page report on an investigation conducted for the last ten months.

Mayor Wagner and Buildings Commissioner Peter J. Reidy

Throgs Neck Bridge Is Opening Today; Bronx Delays Seen

By ROBERT CONLEY

The Throgs Neck Bridge, connecting the Bronx and Queens, will be opened to traffic today.

The $92,000,000 suspension bridge, which crosses the East River at the head of Long Island Sound, is designed mainly to siphon off some of the heavy traffic on the Bronx-Whitestone and Triborough Bridges, farther down river.

It also will open an additional gateway between Long Island and expressways leading to New England, upstate New York, New Jersey and points south and west.

The new bridge and its approaches form the shape of a reverse S. Three lanes of traffic

---

llion Total in Refunds ected by April 15— 61 Cut Is in Doubt

ERNOR LAUDS POLICY

crats in the Assembly ect but G. O. P. Bill asses by 141 to 7

VARREN WEAVER Jr.
ecial to The New York Times.

BANY, Jan. 10—The 1960 income tax was cut 10 nt today.

move will save the state's ers about $90,000,000. or Rockefeller has ex-d doubt that the cut can eated next year.

Governor signed an ad-ration bill making the tax effective at a brief, ul ceremony in his office the afternoon. It had given final approval by ssembly less than two before.

a formal statement after g, Mr. Rockefeller said fund had been made pos-"by good business, good ment and a fair income structure in New York "

0,000,000 Surplus Due

Governor noted in the ent that he anticipated plus of "more than $90,-0" for the fiscal year that ose March 31. Earlier, at s conference, he had said urplus might run as high 5,000,000. The state tax s are due April 15.

Assembly's approval came Democrats had debated st the tax rebate for two Most of them ultimately for it after efforts to it failed. The vote was 7. All the negative votes from Democrats.

Gets Plan for Healt for Aging and Ap High Treasury I

Special to The New York T
WASHINGTON, Ja
President-elect John F. I spent this afternoon di problems of the balance national payments, the budget and space explor

He conferred at the with Secretary Robert son for almost an hou half, and then brief Douglas Dillon, the S designate, and Henry H who was named Unde tary today.

From the Treasury nedy went to the office President-elect Lyndon son, where he met with that has been preparin policy recommendations

Mr. Kennedy's aftern followed a busy mor meeting advisers and reports in New York.

Health Plan Prope

A task force recomm broadened health care aged plan to cover 1 persons. It would be tied to the Social Security and would be financed in the payroll levy on e and employes.

At the same time, seven work groups at tional Conference on H voted for medical car Social Security. The sev opposed.

The President-elect c pre-inaugural headqua New York shortly aft and headed for Palm Be with a stop here. He le ington by plane at 8:5 He is expected to rema parents' home in Palr until he comes to the ca a talk with Presiden hower on Jan. 19 and guration the next day.

Talk With Ander

GEORGIA LOSES AT COURT: Attorney General Eugene Cook, left, and Charles Allen, aide to Gov. S. Ernest Vandiver Jr., at Supreme Court in Washington after petitioning for stay of integration at the University of Georgia. The request was unanimously denied.

2 NEGRO STUDENTS ENTER GEORGIA U.

Integration Effected as U.S. Court Blocks Governor's Effort to Shut School

By CLAUDE SITTON
Special to The New York Times.

ATHENS, Ga., Jan. 10—Two Negroes enrolled in the University of Georgia today after Gov. S. Ernest Vandiver Jr. had been enjoined from cutting off funds and forcing the school to close.

Some 2,000 white students ringed the Academic Building while the two paid their tuition fees, thus completing registration and becoming full-fledged students at the university.

Multi-Nation Bond Issue Payable in 17 Currencies

By EDWIN L. DALE Jr.
Special to The New York Times.

PARIS, Jan. 10—A new financial device will be put into operation in Western Europe later this month. Citizens in five countries will be offered $10,000,000 worth of bonds of a large Portuguese company, denominated in a new international "unit of account" instead of in any national currency.

The buyer will be able to pay for his bonds in any one of six currencies and collect his coupons, as they become due, in any one of seventeen currencies, all European. He will have protection against currency devaluations.

The plan is a major attempt to break the "capital barrier" and thus to enable individual

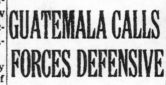

GUATEMALA CALLS FORCES DEFENSIVE

Denies U.S.-Aided Military Preparations Are Aimed at Offensive Against Castro

By JACK RAYMOND

Ambassador
Statement B
for New

BOTH SIDES

Vientiane Re
Invasion by
North Viet

By WILLIAM
Special to The
WASHINGTO
The Soviet G
sented to the U
day a statemen
the situation in
Moscow was
attacked the l
Government in
Premier Boun
was the produ
fluence particu
ence of the Un
The Soviet U
vanna Phoum
Premier now
bodia, as head
Government.
[Meanwhile,
the Boun Ou
asserted tha
North Vietnam
invaded the co
officials were
report.]

Control G
Diplomatic
ington assumed
Ambassador h
Moscow's call
of participants
eva meeting
fighting in Ind
Laos, and divic
the Communist
Communist So
The question
in Laos is the
ernment has th
agreement on
power control
help end the f
Premier Boun
would welcon

1961

Day-o, Day-o, Freedom. Give us freedom.
Freedom's coming and it won't be long.
—Civil rights movement freedom song to the tune of Harry Belafonte's "Day-O"

The year 1961 was one of the busiest and bloodiest years of the young civil rights movement. It was a year that tested the nonviolent commitment of young activists, even as doors long shut were forced open and young people like myself walked through them. It was the year Barack Hussein Obama was born.

On January 9, 1961, I, along with my mother, Vernon Jordan, and Hamp and his father, Alfred "Tup" Holmes, walked through the black iron arch onto the sprawling campus of the University of Georgia. I hadn't really focused on what to expect, even though I had vague memories of the students younger than me who had integrated Little Rock High School in 1957 and had read about Ruby Bridges in New Orleans. They had to walk a gauntlet of white women and men who had screamed at them and called them names, and threatened to lynch them. I remembered how they held their heads high and ignored the threats and white women with their little children in tow who spat on them. On this day, I knew I could do no less.

Facing page: Hamilton Holmes and I were surrounded by newsmen when we arrived on the Athens campus of the University of Georgia on January 9, 1961.

Previous pages: *The New York Times* front page from January 11, 1961. For full text of Georgia University article, see page 154.

I also kept in mind my friends who were putting their lives on the line every day in Atlanta, as well as other students demonstrating throughout the South. Somehow, I believed they were in much greater danger than I. And so I kept focused on getting inside that building and getting registered. I couldn't stretch my mind much beyond that moment.

I was also comforted by the presence of my mother. She was soft-spoken and gave the appearance of being shy, yet she was anything but. In her own quiet way, she had encouraged me from the beginning and never once showed any fear, though she had good reason to be afraid—she knew the dangers of what we were doing. But her quiet support gave me the comfort I needed.

Sure enough, we were greeted by a raucous crowd made up of some of the 20,000 white students at UGA. They limited their violence to words, calling out things like, "There go the niggers." But that didn't bother me. In my mind's eye, I could see myself all those many years ago being crowned queen. And when I heard those hateful words from the crowd, I found myself looking around for the "nigger," since I knew it wasn't me. I knew who I was. I was a queen.

We only had a few feet to go, once we walked under the arch at the entrance, to get to the old white colonial-style building that housed the registrar's office. Inside the building, there was nothing like the scene outside. We were expected and were ushered into a room to begin the registration process, but then we were told we needed to go to the journalism building to finish.

Vernon Jordan and I set out toward the journalism building at a clip so fast that my mother, who was about five feet four inches tall, called out to Vernon, who was over six feet, and me, who was five feet eight, telling us we were walking too fast for her short legs. Vernon and I laughed and slowed down.

It was about a five-minute walk to the building that housed the Henry W. Grady School of Journalism, and as we approached, I experienced a wave of excitement. To be sure, some from the boisterous crowd that had greeted us upon our arrival followed us and began to assemble near the building. But I was immediately caught up in the building itself. There was something so majestic about

Hamp's father, Alfred "Tup" Holmes, led the way as Hamp and I walked to the registrar's office on January 9.

it, with its two towering Romanesque columns and the promise it held for me, that for a moment I felt like any other college student about to take a step toward fulfilling a dream. And when we were met at the door by a bald-headed man with a gentle manner who smiled as if he had a secret, then quietly introduced himself as George Abney, a member of the faculty, I relaxed a little bit more. He then proceeded to discuss my schedule, as he might have with any other student. I shut out the noisy throng of students and reporters that had now gathered outside and even, for a few minutes, my mother and Vernon. But my reverie was broken by the sound of a loud cheer from outside.

The phone rang and Mr. Abney answered it. His expression quickly changed. When he hung up the phone, he informed us that Judge Bootle had granted the state's request to stop the registration. We didn't know why at the time, but we found out later that the judge wrote in his decision that it was to give the state time to "test the correctness" of his desegregation order, although it was never quite clear exactly what that meant. Trying to keep the obvious disappointment from showing on our faces, we walked back through a somewhat tamer crowd, retreating to our cars. Vernon told us that Attorney Hollowell and Attorney Motley, our lawyers in Atlanta, were already headed for the Court of Appeals to get Judge Bootle's ruling overturned. So it was decided we should go to the home of Ray Ware, a local black businessman who had courageously shown us black Southern hospitality during the trial.

I was more exhausted than I realized and fell asleep while waiting for word. Hamp paced the floor. Several hours later, I was awakened by the ringing phone—it was the lawyers in Atlanta telling us the Appeals Court judge, Elbert Tuttle, had overturned the federal judge's ruling. My normally quiet mother shouted, "God is good, isn't he?"

We immediately grabbed up our things and piled out of the Wares' and headed back to the journalism building to finish our registration. By the end of the day, we had become not only the first black students to enroll at the University of Georgia, but the first to successfully desegregate an all-white college anywhere in the South.

Hamp and I left the the administration building after successfully registering (finally).

The next day, my mother went with me to Center Myers Hall, the dormitory where I was to stay. We were met by the house mother, Mrs. Minnie Porter, a kindly gray-haired white woman who didn't act as if there was anything out of the ordinary. After introductions, she led us across the wide lobby area, where students received guests, to the only rooms on the other side. They had been the student government offices, but those had been moved to make room for me, since a decision had been made that I should not be on the floor with the other girls. The two rooms were nice and spacious, with a kitchenette and a full bathroom with a tub. Mrs. Porter was gracious and told us to call her if we needed anything.

Soon after Mrs. Porter left, we decided to go for an early dinner at Killian's, the restaurant owned by the black family Hamilton would be staying with. (As a male, he was not required to live on campus.) We had dinner and got back to the dorm before dark. I knew that sooner or later I would have to say farewell and would begin my time alone, so sooner rather than later, I hugged my mother and said goodbye. She and I both acted as if it was not an out-of-the-ordinary occurrence, and that made it easier for me to retreat back into my room and close the door. Outside, a crowd soon gathered and began chanting things like "Nigger go home." But I was so glad to have reached this stage that I was able to pretty much shut them out. I was also worn out, so I searched around in my suitcase for a pair of pajamas, and without unpacking the rest, I fell into bed and went fast asleep.

But the State and its allies were not yet ready to concede defeat. I went to class, walking and sitting alone for two days. Neither the professors nor the students acknowledged my presence. There was still tension in the air, and students at a distance yelled at me, calling me more ugly racist names. I got used to the crowd that came at night and stood on the grass outside my window chanting things like "Two, four, six, eight. We don't want to integrate." So I proceeded to make myself comfortable in my suite.

On the third night, the crowd erupted into violence. Throughout the day, some students had been spreading the word to continue the protests outside my dormitory, so there was already a crowd gathering. But that night, the Georgia basketball team played a hotly contested game with Georgia Tech, its biggest rival. The game went into an unusual double overtime and ended in a loss for the university. The frustration of losing the game led to even more students wanting to let off steam, so they all headed up the hill to my dorm and joined those who were already there. We later found out that there were adults in the crowd egging the students on, and that the lieutenant governor of Georgia, Peter Zack Geer, had called to encourage the students to protest.

The white girls on the second floor had also been told to turn off their lights so my room would be the only one with lights and therefore easy to locate. I was sitting at the vanity when suddenly I heard a crash. I turned to look, and the first thing I saw was glass spattered all over the clothes in my open suitcase. Then I saw the brick lying on top of the glass. My first thought was: *So this is what it's like in the middle of a riot.* It was kind of what they say the eye of a hurricane is like; while the wind is blowing ferociously in swirling gusts, at the center of this terrifying movement all is calm. And that's how I felt. I called my mother to tell her not to turn on the television because if she did, she would worry and that there was no need. I was safe.

I was confident that no harm would come to me. I reached back into a space my grandmother, Alberta Hunter, had created when I used to spend my summers in Florida with her and my grandfather "Shep," a presiding elder preacher in the African Methodist Episcopal Church. She was very spiritual and insisted that I learn verses from the Bible, including her favorite, the Twenty-third Psalm. Although I could hear the ugliness from outside, I could also hear: "Yea though I walk through the valley of the shadow of death, I shall fear no evil. Thy rod and thy staff they comfort me all the days of my life."

It had been a long time since I learned those words, but they were coming to me now at probably the most important time in my life. And, in fact, no physical harm *did* come. Within a short while the dean arrived and told me that Hamp and I were being suspended for our own safety. It was a ruse that had been successful in an earlier integration effort in Alabama, when its first black student, Autherine Lucy, was suspended, never to return.

By the time the dean got to my room, the police had also arrived and begun dispersing the crowd with tear gas. But they had taken their time getting there. All the other students had been told to remove their sheets since the tear gas might linger there and cause their eyes to tear. As I walked through the lobby, I passed by a semicircle of the white girls from upstairs, and one threw a quarter in my direction. "Here's a quarter, Charlayne," she called. "Go upstairs and change my sheets."

At this point, I had not met any of the white students in my dorm, so my first impressions were based on the behavior of those girls.

Hamp had not heard about the riot, but state highway patrolmen had arrived at his place by the time I got there in the dean's car. When he learned that we were being taken back to Atlanta, Hamp wanted to drive the new little Opel his grandfather had given him, and was being pretty adamant about it. Even though the men who were there were uniformed state officers of the law, I was afraid they might be of the same mind as many of the policemen in other Southern states who had aided the segregationists who attacked nonviolent protestors. I also worried that if Hamp were driving alone, an "accident" might be made to happen and no one could prove otherwise. I resorted to the one thing I knew would help change his mind: I started jumping up and down and loudly and

The window of my dorm room, smashed by rioters on my third night at the University of Georgia. One brick landed in the suitcase at the foot of my bed!

repeatedly shouting, "You can't drive. It's too dangerous." As I knew he would, Hamp, who was very well behaved, found my loud shouting embarrassing, so he gave in and the two of us were spirited away from Athens in the dark of night in the backseat of a Georgia state patrol car.

Even with Hamp in the car, I was a bit concerned about traveling that highway, since many of the small towns along the way were home to Ku Klux Klanners and other white supremacists. But we made it to Atlanta safely and went straight to my house, where Hamp's father, Attorney Hollowell, and Carl Holman had come to meet us. My mother was standing at the door when we arrived and took us both in her arms and held us tight. By the following day, Hollowell and his co-counsel Constance Baker Motley, had won still another court ruling, ordering us back. The adults decided we should use the weekend to catch our breath and be refreshed by the support of the community. In the interim, a white man carrying a gun showed up at my dormitory in Athens asking for me. But he was escorted out and not heard from again. We later learned he had escaped from an insane asylum.

On Monday, we returned to campus. And for all practical purposes, that was the end of the active resistance to our presence. From time to time, students would let the air out of the tires of one or the other of our cars, and on one occasion someone scraped "nigger" across the driver's side door of Hamp's car. Students also shouted unpleasant things as we walked by, especially when some civil rights action somewhere else was occurring—like the Freedom Rides. Those protests resonated like minor aftershocks from a faraway earthquake. I remember walking across campus one day and hearing a white student yell out "Freedom Rider" as I passed. To my ears, that was the highest praise.

The Freedom Riders of 1961 also stood on the shoulders of giants. Their purpose was to test the enforcement of desegregation on interstate bus routes. Thanks to earlier NAACP plaintiffs, the U.S. Supreme Court had spoken on three separate occasions affirming desegregation orders. The Supreme Court cases established the primacy of federal law over state law and custom—the contest that would be waged in other areas throughout the years of civil rights movement.

New York Times.

LATE CITY EDITION

U. S. Weather Bureau Report (Page 95) forecasts:
Variable cloudiness today and tonight. Rather cloudy tomorrow.
Temp. range: 66—50; yesterday: 70—50.

SECTION ONE

NEW YORK, SUNDAY, MAY 21, 1961.

35c outside New York City, its suburban area and Long Island.
50c in 17 Western states, Canada; higher in air delivery cities.

THIRTY CENTS

HEV GIVES ER GOODS ROLE NOW

dicates Soviet Emphasis in al Production

D CARUTHERS
ne New York Times.

May 20 — Premier aid today his Gov-beginning to turn ation to consumer uld no longer give the production of ry.

consider our heavy built," Mr. Khru-red at a reception ficials and exhibi-arge British Trade pened in Moscow

not going to give remier Khrushchev light industry and ry will develop at e."

et leader's im-arks indicated that level off the de-heavy and light already been made. ean a considerable the original project e seven-year plan d in 1965.

anges Predicted
ions were that the a shifted em-duction was being studied by Mr. and his aides in for the twenty-sec-ss of the Soviet party at which dramatic changes .

Soviet consumers steady but gradual the last few years ability of clothing y household goods. e distribution sys-kes ordinary neces-t to get and, prices

Khrushchev had by some of the

KOREA PRESIDENT RETURNS TO POST; CABINET SWORN IN

Coup Leader Now Premier —Action by Yun Eases Seoul Legal Situation

By BERNARD KALB
Special to The New York Times.

SEOUL, Korea, Sunday, May 21—Military rule was formally introduced in South Korea to-day with the swearing in of a Cabinet of fourteen men, all from the armed forces.

The legal path for the new Government was cleared when President Posun Yun resumed late yesterday the post as head of state that he had resigned Friday.

The Cabinet pledged firmness in meeting the national crisis and vowed to strengthen the re-public's ties with the United Nations.

Chang in Defense Post

The Cabinet, hand-picked by the military junta that rose to power in a coup here early Tuesday, replaces the Cabinet of Premier John M. Chang. Dr. Chang, elected to office last August, resigned under pres-sure Thursday.

Heading the new Government is Lieut. Gen. Chang Do Young, the 38-year-old Army Chief of Staff. General Chang, who led the coup, also becomes Min-ister of Defense.

General Chang in a speech to the ministers told them to di-rect all their energies and ef-forts toward the earliest reali-zation of the goals of the revo-lution—the nation's economic and political reform, a stepped-up fight on communism and the eventual unification of Korea.

New Government's Pledge

As the new Cabinet under General Chang was installed, each Minister took an oath as follows:

"I do solemnly pledge to the people that I will concentrate my efforts upon strengthening national power for the unifica-

---

400 U.S. MARSHALS SENT TO ALABAMA AS MONTGOMERY BUS RIOTS HURT 20, PRESIDENT BIDS STATE KEEP ORDER

Associated Press Wirephoto
ALABAMA STREET SCENE: A Negro student, who arrived in Montgomery aboard bus carrying anti-segregation riders from Birmingham, being beaten yesterday by white men.

THREAT SILENCES MIGRANT WITNESS

U. S. Hearings on Farming Workers End Here With Testimony on Abuses

---

Freedom Riders Attacked By Whites in Montgomery

By The Associated Press.

MONTGOMERY, Ala, May 20—Street fighting that left at least twenty persons beaten with clubs and fists raged for two hours here today after a white mob had attacked a busload of Freedom Riders.

The fighting broke out and **NEGROES FACING**

FORCE DUE TODA

Agents to Bear Arm —Injunction Sough Against the Klan

Texts of U. S. and Alabam statements on Page 78.

By ANTHONY LEWIS
Special to The New York Times.

WASHINGTON, May 20 The Federal Government di patched 400 marshals and armed officers to Alabama t night to restore order in are that were torn by racial vi lence.

The Government acted aft a mob of white persons at tacked a racially mixed gro of bus riders in Montgome Ala. The disorders lasted tv hours. At least twenty of tl riders were beaten.

Attorney General Robert Kennedy announced the Fe eral action in a telegram Alabama officials. He said was necessary to "guarant safe passage in interstate co merce."

Marshals Due by Noon

The 400 Federal marshals w be in Montgomery by noon t morrow, a Justice Departme spokesman said. He said th would have arm bands for idc tification and would carry sic arms as well as tear-gas bom and riot clubs or night sticks.

Mr. Kennedy disclosed a that he would ask the Fede Court in Montgomery "to enjc the Ku Klux Klan, the Nation States Rights Party, certain dividuals and all persons acti in concert with them from terfering with peaceful int

---

New York Times front page from May 21, 1961. For full text of bus riots article, see page 156.

The first of the interstate civil rights rulings came in 1946 and involved Irene Morgan, who made history by refusing to give up her seat on a bus from Hayes Store, Virginia, to Baltimore. When Morgan lost her case in the Virginia Supreme Court, the twenty-seven-year-old single mother enlisted the assistance of NAACP lawyers Spottswood Robinson, Oliver Hill, and Martin A. Martin. After hearing their case, the U.S. Supreme Court overruled the Virginia Supreme Court on June 3, 1946.

In the same year, James Farmer, then with the Fellowship of Reconciliation, an interracial social justice organization, and later one of the founders of the Congress of Racial Equality (CORE), led an interracial group of sixteen on what he called a Journey of Reconciliation. They boarded buses and traveled to some fifteen Southern cities and found that they all maintained segregated facilities in defiance of the Supreme Court ruling. Some of the riders even got arrested and sent to jail for breaking the laws of those states.

But Southern custom continued to prevail. That meant separate waiting rooms in bus stations for whites and blacks, and separate facilities on the bus, where blacks had to sit in the back while whites occupied the front seats. I remember before I reached my teens traveling with my grandmother from Atlanta to New York, and sitting in the segregated section of the train. My grandmother knew we could not get served on the long, overnight train ride, so she prepared food—fried chicken, boiled eggs, homemade cookies, cake, and other food that wouldn't perish. I made many friends from all over the South on such trips, and we shared our food. Blacks had learned how to make the best of a bad situation.

In 1953, still another case went to the Supreme Court, this time with major legal consequences. It was the case of Sarah Keys, a black army private who was forced to give up her bus seat to a white marine in Roanoke Rapids, North Carolina. The U.S. Supreme Court handed down its affirmative decision in 1955, six days before Rosa Parks refused to give up her seat on a bus in Montgomery, Alabama. The *Keys* case extended the 1954 *Brown* decision outlawing "separate but equal" segregation in public education to include interstate transport.

Then, in 1960, a Howard University law student, Bruce Boynton, was arrested for attempting to desegregate the Trailways bus terminal restaurant in Richmond, Virginia. In its ruling, the Supreme Court extended its order to include bus stations and toilets used by interstate passengers. It was this ruling and the ferment that was building from the sit-ins and other protests in the South that in 1961 moved James Farmer, now the new director of CORE, to put the "movement on wheels" to challenge Jim Crow. The plan was to draw attention to illegal segregation by having blacks and whites travel together, sitting side by side and in the front of the bus where local law prohibited blacks from doing so. They would attempt to be served in the segregated restaurants in bus stations and use the restrooms. According to Farmer, their short-term goal was similar to that of the students involved in sit-ins: "to provoke the southern authorities into arresting us and thereby prod the Justice Department into enforcing the law of the land." Arrests would once again put federal law to the test. Activists like James Lawson, who trained students in nonviolence and helped prepare them for this dangerous mission, believed that federal officials—"adversaries," he called them—were afraid of upsetting Southern white voters by challenging the segregated stations, so instead they turned a blind eye. In this case, Lawson argued that the Freedom Rides were not really civil disobedience, but "merely what the Supreme Court said we had a right to do." Freedom Rides would test both the law and the commitment of newly elected president John F. Kennedy to end segregation.

Just as the sit-in demonstrators had been prepared, the Freedom Riders also had a week of training in how to protect themselves nonviolently in case of attack. It was to come in handy.

A mixed group of thirteen blacks and whites, including John Lewis, who was by now a sit-in veteran, got ready to ride. On May 4, they divided into two groups, one taking the Greyhound Bus Line and the other Trailways, from Washington, D.C., to New Orleans. They planned on arriving on May 17, in time for a planned celebration of the seven-year anniversary of the Supreme Court's

James Farmer, director of CORE, joined the Freedom Riders at a lunch counter sit-in at the bus station in Montgomery, Alabama, on May 24, 1961.

school desegregation decision. They knew that what they were about to do could well result in violence against them. Lewis remembered: "We were prepared to die. Some of us signed letters and wills. We didn't know whether we would return."

The riders also notified the federal government of their intentions. The notification challenged federal agents to protect them, but could also expose their willful inaction—in some cases of violence against protestors, agents had known in advance and had done nothing or even colluded with the segregationists.

After traveling through several Southern states, the group encountered their first violence in Rock Hill, South Carolina. A crowd of white toughs who frequented the bus station's pinball machines were not waiting on the Freedom Riders, but when John Lewis stepped off the Greyhound bus and attempted to enter through the white entrance, one of the whites directed him to the colored entrance. Lewis responded, "I have a right to go in here on grounds of the Supreme Court decision in the Boynton case." One of the white youths spat out a profanity, and when Lewis ignored it and started in through the door, a young white man punched him in the mouth, thus giving Lewis the dubious distinction of taking the first blow to a Freedom Rider.

When other attackers proceeded to beat Lewis, Albert Bigelow, a white Freedom Rider, stepped in between them and was beaten to the ground. So was Genevieve Hughes, a female Freedom Rider. But battered, bruised, and bleeding, they all got up and refused to press charges against their attackers. Some two hours later, the Trailways bus arrived, but the station was closed.

That night, both sets of riders met at Friendship Junior College, in Rock Hill, and the next day, they continued on to Georgia and passed through Athens, where they stopped and had lunch. Their stop was so uneventful I never knew they had come so close to where I was attending classes, nor did anyone else in Athens. They ended up that night in Atlanta where, after their journey of 700 miles, they had dinner with Dr. King. The two groups then continued in their separate buses to Alabama.

When the Greyhound bus group got to Anniston, Alabama, a white mob of some fifty men "carrying metal pipes, clubs and chains . . . milled around menacingly, some screaming, 'Dirty Communists' and 'Sieg Heil.'" They included a former ex-convict and Ku Klux Klansman, Roger Crouch, and Anniston Klan leader William Chappell. But the door was boarded shut by two Alabama state patrolmen—Corporals Ell Cowling and Harry Sims—who had been riding the bus undercover and secretly taping the riders so they could inform the governor

Freedom Riders narrowly escaped when their Greyhound bus was attacked and set on fire by local residents outside Anniston, Alabama, on May 14. This photograph of the burning bus got world-wide attention.

and the head of the state patrol of their plans. Rising anger led the white attackers to slash the bus tires. But the passengers directed the bus driver to pull out, and he readily complied. The bus only got a short distance out of Anniston before the slashed tires went flat. The driver jumped off the bus and ran into a nearby grocery store and began calling local garages to try to find new tires. The other passengers remained as the mob outside attacked the bus with bricks and an ax, breaking the windows. When they couldn't open the door, they began shouting "Burn them alive" and "Fry the goddam niggers," and threw a firebomb into the bus, forcing the coughing passengers to try to escape.

The mob changed its tactic. Instead of trying to get into the bus, they now moved to trap the Freedom Riders inside. One of the state investigators drew his gun and forced the crowd away from the door. As the riders emerged, they were set upon. Hank Thomas, the first rider to get off the bus, was hit in the head with a baseball bat and knocked to the ground, "barely conscious as the rest of the exiting riders spilled out onto the grass."

Eventually, Alabama state troopers appeared, and the mob fled. But in this single moment, the Freedom Riders had a major achievement: the photograph of the burning bus, with plumes of thick black smoke rising into the clear blue sky, played in the media around the world, drawing attention to the cause as never before. A handful of whites from a nearby neighborhood came to the aid of the Freedom Riders and, as author Ray Arsenault recalled, a twelve-year-old white girl, Janie Miller, "supplied the choking victims with water, filling and refilling a

National Guard soldiers escort Freedom Riders from Montgomery, Alabama, to Jackson, Mississippi, on May 24.

five-gallon bucket while braving the insults and taunts of the Klansmen." She and her family were so ostracized they had to move out of the area.

Despite the public relations victory following the bus burning, the Freedom Riding foot soldiers were still in grave danger, as the Trailways bus passengers found out when they arrived in Anniston, unaware of what had just happened to the Greyhound. In no time, they too were under attack. A group of pro-segregationist whites climbed onto the bus in the Anniston station. Two Atlanta college students—Morris Brown sophomore Herbert Harris and Charles Person, a fresh-man from Morehouse, were the first casualties. As the passengers began to recite their right under the Supreme Court order to sit at the front of the bus, Person was hit in the face. Then he and Harris were thrown into the aisle as the mob kicked and hit them. Walter Bergman, a retired professor from Michigan, moved to stop the beatings, but the mob resented him even more because he was white. They beat him so badly that he ultimately required fifty-three stitches on his head. (He later had a stroke, becoming paralyzed for life.) The whites took seats in the middle of the bus to make sure the blacks stayed in the back as the bus continued on to Birmingham.

By the time the Trailways bus got to Birmingham, another mob had gath-ered. Bloodied but unbowed, the riders got off and headed for the white waiting room. By an earlier agreement, Birmingham police had let the mob know they would have fifteen minutes to attack the Freedom Riders before the police inter-vened. The crowd set upon all of the riders with vicious blows to their faces and bodies. They also turned their violence on journalists and anyone else they didn't recognize, including other whites. Most of the Trailways riders eventually escaped and caught taxis that took them to the home of Fred Shuttlesworth, a local minister who was the head of the Alabama Christian Movement for Human Rights. But the fear was so great that one black doctor refused to treat young Person, and some hospitals turned away even the most severely injured. James Peck, a white Freedom Rider, eventually had to have some fifty stitches to close a gash across his forehead and cuts on his face.

In the national scrutiny that followed, Alabama governor John Patterson was defiant, saying, "We cannot act as nursemaids to agitators; the state of Alabama can't guarantee the safety of fools." When Bull Connor, the white police chief of Birmingham, was asked by a journalist why there had been no police protection for the riders, Connor responded that the police had all been visiting their mothers. It was Mother's Day.

After the violence in Birmingham, bus drivers refused to take the Freedom Riders any farther, so the original riders decided to head to New Orleans by air, in time for the May 17 celebration. No sooner had they left than a group from the Nashville movement decided to take their place. They, too, left letters to be mailed "in case they were killed." Instead of being killed, they were arrested in Birmingham on May 17. Among them was the now more-than-once battered John Lewis, who joined the group in jail on a hunger strike. But in the predawn hours the following morning, Bull Connor and several of his policemen forced the students out of the jail and drove them about 120 miles, dropping them somewhere near a railroad track in a part of Tennessee the riders knew nothing about. When they finally stumbled upon a house where they could use a telephone, they called Diane Nash in Nashville. She told them that others had left to join the Freedom Ride in Birmingham. So the intrepid group went back to Birmingham, where they made plans to travel on to Montgomery.

By this time, a federal official named John Seigenthaler had met with Governor John Patterson in an attempt to negotiate safe passage for the Freedom Riders. But despite Seigenthaler's efforts, the governor refused to talk with either Attorney General Robert F. Kennedy or his brother President John F. Kennedy. Seigenthaler did secure a promise from Washington that the Freedom Riders would be protected from Birmingham to the city limits of Montgomery, where he had been told the city police would take over.

On May 20, the students boarded a Greyhound bus and left town, with thirty-two patrol cars traveling in front of and behind them. But some forty miles outside Montgomery, the visible state protection disappeared. And when the buses hit Montgomery, upward of a thousand angry whites descended on them with baseball bats, clubs, and chains. White women used their pocketbooks as weapons. Even

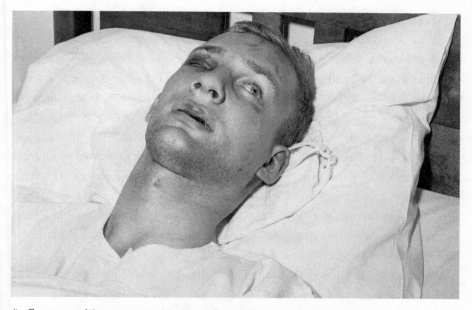

Jim Zwerg, one of the more seriously wounded Riders, recuperated in a Montgomery hospital on May 21.

the federal government's representative, John Seigenthaler, was attacked and knocked unconscious as he tried to rescue two white women from the mayhem.

Jim Zwerg, one of the original white Freedom Riders, was attacked, kicked in the groin, face, and ribs. Later from a hospital bed, Zwerg related another dramatic story that helped put the Freedom Riders and their cause on the international conscience. Looking as if he had been on a battlefield in a war zone, Zwerg managed to speak these words: "Segregation must be stopped. It must be broken down. We're going on to New Orleans no matter what. We're dedicated to this. We'll take the hitting. We'll take the beating." And given the wounds on his swollen face, he was convincing when he said, "We're willing to accept death."

Later that evening, activists gathered for a rally in the church of an SCLC stalwart, Reverend Ralph Abernathy. But the group grew increasingly concerned about the growing number of angry whites ringing the church outside.

Inexperienced federal marshals finally arrived, and as the crowd grew more agitated, the marshals responded by throwing canisters of tear gas. But the noxious gas flew into the wind. Violence followed and even today, when John Lewis recalls that night, he breaks down: "Had it not been for President Kennedy federalizing the National Guard and putting the city under martial law, I think many of us would have been killed in that church on that night. It was a scary night."

That night, Martin Luther King, with Lewis by his side, held a press conference in the Rev. Abernathy's living room. Many local blacks wanted to retaliate against the white population for the violence at Abernathy's church. Dr. King argued against that, saying: "This is a testing point . . . We don't want to do that. We have won the moral victory." He also said, "We think we are doing a great service to our nation, for this is not a struggle for ourselves alone, but a struggle for the soul of America . . . The time is always right to do right."

Despite the ineptness of the federal marshals, the Freedom Riders and others got out of Montgomery alive. Their strategy of nonviolent resistance had worked. It had forced the federal government to protect the activists, who had only been engaging in their rights under federal law, from white segregationists—a role that the government had earlier claimed was not a part of its mandate.

With the eleven from Nashville, the Freedom Riders now numbered twenty-one, and they set out for Jackson, Mississippi. To keep up their spirits, they sang:

> *I'm taking a ride on the Greyhound bus line,*
> *I'm a-riding the front seat to Jackson this time.*
> *Hallelujah, I'm a travelin'*
> *Hallelujah, ain't it fine?*
> *Hallelujah, I'm a travelin'*
> *Down Freedom's main line.*

When they arrived in Jackson, the Freedom Riders walked off the bus and into the arms of the Jackson police. They were taken to jail and later given $200 fines and suspended sixty-day jail sentences. They refused to pay the fines, choosing

After the Riders were badly beaten up in Birmingham on May 20, James Farmer, the Rev. Ralph Abernathy, Dr. Martin Luther King, and the injured John Lewis held a press conference to announce that the rides would continue . . .

instead to work them off in prison, and were sentenced to the infamous maximum-security Parchman prison. By summer's end, more than 300 Freedom Riders had been arrested—more than half were black, a quarter were female, most were Southern college students. They were subjected to harsh conditions in prison, where "the steel was cold and you only had a pair of shorts and a T-shirt on." They sustained themselves by singing freedom songs.

Meanwhile, the wide international coverage of the brutality against the Freedom Riders had moved Attorney General Kennedy to ask the Interstate Commerce Commission for stringent regulations halting segregation in interstate bus terminals and on buses, followed by a federal condemnation of the order of a district judge in Montgomery against the Freedom Rides.

The Freedom Rides were over in that area of the South, but they had left a powerful legacy. They had embarrassed the federal government into doing the right thing: enforcing the law of the land.

Later that year, it was Albany, Georgia's turn. Albany was a semi-rural area, where blacks often disappeared without a trace. It, too, was totally segregated. It was there that seven black and four white Freedom Riders created a coalition of organizations that included local leaders of the black community and members of the SCLC and SNCC. Working together, the coalition organized a full-court press against all aspects of segregation in Albany, arranging sit-ins, boycotts, and marches. They called themselves the Albany Movement.

SNCC did what it did best: organize among the grass roots. But so spontaneous was the birth of the Albany Movement that it made up its plans as it went along, finally calling in Dr. Martin Luther King to help bring attention to their cause. Dr. King had only made plans to speak, fire up the people, and leave. But without consulting him, Dr. William G. Anderson, the movement's leader, announced that Dr. King would be joining them in a march the following day. Though surprised, Dr. King felt he had no choice but to march. He was arrested during a demonstration the next day. Soon, hundreds demonstrated and filled jails in and around Albany, and many were treated brutally. One SNCC leader, Charles Sherrod, recalled being slapped around for not saying "sir" when he responded to a white policeman.

The local police chief, Laurie Pritchett, had studied the Gandhian nonviolence philosophy that informed Dr. King and the Albany Movement and vowed he was going to "out-nonviolent them." Although he made arrests at demonstrations, he made sure his police force abstained from the kind of violence against the marchers that would garner national attention. And he quickly moved jailed protestors to facilities elsewhere in the county, so that his jail was never full.

In one way, Albany was not the most successful challenge of the civil rights movement. There were tensions within the movement about strategies and tactics, as well as leadership, and in the end white promises to desegregate were not kept. Yet, it produced what the movement's leader, William G. Anderson, called "a change in the attitude of the people"—producing "a determination never to accept that segregated society, as it was, anymore."

And the Albany Movement, in a sense, served as a training ground for future movement activities, as organizers learned what worked and what didn't. It also produced songs of freedom that gave a lift to the brutalized freedom fighters and which were heard by an increasingly sympathetic world. It was here that the seeds were sown for the harmonies of the later world-renowned *a cappella* group Sweet Honey in the Rock. In so many ways, as SNCC's Charles Sherrod said, "We showed the world."

That summer, I returned to Atlanta after a three-month summer internship at the *Louisville Courier Journal and Times.* It had been a fantastic experience for me. I had convinced the editors to let me try my hand in the field, and before the summer was over, they had published several of my stories, featuring them prominently, sometimes with photographs, in the paper. Once back home, I immediately began putting what I had learned into my work at the *Inquirer,* which by then had established itself as what *Time* magazine would call a "loud voice in Atlanta." *Time* wrote that the *Inquirer* was "neither a good newspaper nor a financial success . . . often badly written, amateurish in its approach. As far as the *Inquirer* is concerned, the only important stories are those involving the Negroes' aggressive pursuit of equality. But in this electric sector of human endeavor, the *Inquirer* is giving lessons to newspapers all over the South."

I wrote what I thought were muckraking stories about the overcrowded conditions in the still-segregated black high schools, as well as the overcrowded and understaffed public hospital—the only option for poor blacks in Atlanta. I spent much of a Saturday night in the hospital's emergency room, where black people who had been shot or stabbed or otherwise injured lay on gurneys in open hallways, unshielded from passersby and reporters like me. I remember one man who had

... and on May 28 they were back—another group of riders staging another sit-in, at a waiting room reserved for whites in Montgomery, Alabama.

been shot and had died from his wounds. I asked one of the white ER doctors where he had been shot. The doctor produced a long, thin wire and proceeded to ram it deep into a hole in the man's head. I had had enough for one night!

I also had my first experience with the power of the press and the white "power structure" when I called the white school superintendent, Ira Jarrell, to ask about the poor condition of the schools for blacks. She actually came to the phone and not only took my questions, but answered them.

It was also the summer when I met Martin Luther King, Jr., for the first time. It was a brief, unplanned meeting on Auburn Avenue, where his father's church, as well as most of the black businesses, were located. There were so many prosperous black businesses on that street, it was called "Sweet Auburn."

I recognized Dr. King as he was surrounded by a group of adults. In my youthful, unabashed enthusiasm, I ran up to him and introduced myself. He said he knew who I was, that I was doing a magnificent job at UGA, and he was proud to meet me. I, for once, was speechless.

That year, Atlanta student demonstrations caused white businessmen to close some seventy downtown lunch counters for three months. But the crisis was later resolved by the involvement of white businessmen and black adult leaders. Although the students were unhappy with the settlement linking desegregation of lunch counters and other public facilities with school desegregation, it was ratified. Still, as I wrote many years later, "freedom and equality was still burning inside them every day as they took up new challenges or managed old ones . . . everywhere any of us went we found gratitude expressed in many ways that kept us inspired."

Meanwhile, as sit-ins continued in many cities and towns across the South, SNCC took a new step in its efforts to end segregation by adding voting rights to its program.

A number of actors contributed to the decision to concentrate on voting rights, including the Kennedy administration, led by Robert Kennedy. He argued that Freedom Rides had gone as far as they could go, and it was time to engage in what Kennedy called a chance to change the face of the South.

Bob Moses was one of the earliest SNCC members to take that leap, first venturing in the summer heat into some of the most dangerous territory in the Deep South—McComb, Mississippi.

The state of Mississippi has a complex history. In the mid-nineteenth century, it imported a quarter of a million slaves to work its fields. African slaves, who knew how to till the soil, were brought there, and their labor made the area very profitable for its owners. In the Delta, in the northwest section of the state, cotton flourished.

After the Civil War, blacks flocked to the region and profited for a brief while as farmers. They also held political office. The first black man to serve in the U.S. Congress, Hiram Roberts, hailed from Mississippi, and so did Blanche K. Bruce, who served in the U.S. Senate from 1875 to 1881. No other African American would serve in the Senate until 1966.

But for blacks, the prosperity—economic and political—was short-lived. In 1890, the state began imposing onerous literacy tests that required potential voters to recite and later interpret portions of the Mississippi constitution to the satisfaction of the white registrar, who sometimes could not read or write himself. The state also imposed a poll tax, which required potential black voters to pay for the privilege of voting. Voters also had to be "of good character," determined by the white registrar, and their names had to be published for two consecutive weeks in a newspaper of general circulation. These were major barriers to blacks, especially having their names and addresses published in a climate where whites did not hesitate to harass or even kill blacks they saw as "uppity."

Black leaders like the NAACP's Amzie Moore and C. C. Bryant had been pressing for a voting rights campaign since the 1940s. They shared the belief that voting was the key to black liberation in Mississippi. So when they learned that SNCC was getting into voting rights, Bryant invited the young SNCC activist Bob Moses to the Pike County Mississippi town of McComb. In July 1961, Moses arrived, and with the help of NAACP activists, they set up a voter education program there. At that time, only five percent of blacks were registered.

Moses had no experience in the Deep South. He was a Harlem-born, Harvard-trained student of philosophy and a high school teacher in New York City. But, "when he saw the pictures of students sitting-in at Southern lunch counters, he said: 'They looked like I felt.'" Despite the differences between the NAACP and SNCC, the two organizations had a good working relationship. Amzie Moore, in fact, helped Moses understand not only the psyche of the people he lived among and wanted to help advance, but also the mentality of local whites.

At Moore's suggestion, Moses set up voter registration classes in McComb at the Masonic Temple. The classes were modeled after a program that had been set up in the 1950s in South Carolina by Septima Clark, a teacher and activist who, in Andrew Young's words, "made the Civil Rights Movement possible," and taught blacks how to read and write, and to fill out things like driver's license applications and voter registration forms, and to pass the voter registration test.

The soft-spoken Moses went ahead with an almost messianic devotion to his work. More than once, he was assaulted and jailed on trumped-up charges. Against the advice of older blacks in McComb who said it was too dangerous, Moses ventured into the remote rural areas like Amite County. Most African Americans there were so afraid that, as Taylor Branch, an author who has chronicled Dr. King and the civil rights movement, recalled, it sometimes took Moses a half day to find a place to spend the night.

Eventually, Moses convinced three African American volunteers to come with him to the Amite county courthouse. They were elated to be on their way to fill out voter registration forms. But not for long. They were followed by a patrolman, who pulled them over, and when Moses asked why, the patrolman arrested him on a charge of interfering with an officer in the discharge of his duties. Moses was later released after national NAACP officials came and paid his bail. But a few weeks later, Moses tried again. He didn't pressure the black men who came to his talks on registration, but eventually two volunteered.

"The next morning, August 29, the three of them found the sidewalk near the courthouse blocked by three young white men," wrote Taylor Branch, who described the scene this way: "Dawson recognized the one in front as Billy Jack Caston, the second was another of the sheriff's cousins, and the third was the sheriff's son. There was very little talk. Caston asked Moses where he was going. To the registrar's office, Moses replied. Caston said no he wasn't and struck a quick, swiping blow to Moses's forehead with the handle of his knife."

Caston continued hitting Moses's head and slammed it into the pavement, where he hit him again. Despite the beating (Moses later required nine stitches to sew up three head wounds), Moses's commitment to nonviolence kept him from fighting back physically. He fought back in his own way, by regaining his feet and continuing to the registrar's office with his two volunteers. The registrar closed the office rather than entertain their requests. The next day, Moses filed a complaint against his attacker, but to no avail. Caston was acquitted by an all-white jury.

On September 25, Herbert Lee, a fifty-two-year-old father of nine, who had volunteered to drive Moses around the county, was shot and killed by E. H.

Hurst, a white member of the Mississippi legislature who claimed he had fired in self-defense. Initially Louis Allen, a black man who saw what happened, corroborated Hurst's story. But later, Allen summoned the courage to tell the truth. He would also be murdered before he could testify about the intimidation that had led to his false testimony.

Despite the risks, Moses's volunteers continued to work to register black voters. One volunteer was sixteen-year-old Brenda Travis, who later got arrested sitting in at McComb's Greyhound bus station. The local authorities put her in jail with adult criminals. When she was released and tried to return to school, the conservative black principal, whose position was at the mercy of white school administrators, suspended her and another student who had participated in the sit-in. But Travis was undeterred, not least because about a hundred students walked out behind them. The high school students had the freedom fever and leaped out ahead of their fearful parents, and in some cases, even the young SNCC officials like Moses and SNCC chairman Charles McDew. Moses and McDew tried but were unable to contain the younger students when they decided to march on the courthouse where Travis and the other students had been sentenced to eight months in jail for "breech of peace." (Brenda was singled out for harsher treatment: she got a year in the state school for delinquents.) The courthouse was a few miles away, and so as night fell, the marchers diverted to the McComb County City Hall. There they were confronted by a crowd of whites. Nevertheless, the students walked one by one to the steps and began to pray. All, including Brenda Travis, were arrested, but not before Moses and McDew and Bob Zellner, the lone white among the protestors, were severely beaten by the mob. One attacker tried to gouge out Zellner's eyes. (White SNCC members were even more despised than black members.)

As Zellner recalled:

> One of the guys got behind me . . . he started putting his fingers into my eye sockets and he actually would work my eyeball out of my eye socket and sort of down on my cheekbone. . . . He was trying to get my

eyeball between his thumb and his index finger so he could get a grip on it and really pull it out. So what I would do is, I would wait until he had maneuvered it into a good place and before he could clamp down, I would move my head in such a way that it would make him lose his grip. And my eyeball would slip between his fingers and pop back in my head, with a thunk.

Still, the students had succeeded in launching the first major civil rights demonstration in Mississippi history, and it stirred many of their parents to support, if not to action.

"Where the students lead, we will follow," declared C. C. Bryant, the head of the Pike County NAACP.

Brenda Travis was sentenced to an indefinite term in the state reform school. The other arrested students were not allowed back in school unless they signed pledges not to demonstrate anymore. The students responded by picketing the school. For its part, SNCC started a school for them and called it Nonviolent High. It closed when the SNCC teachers were sentenced to four to six months in prison. At that point, some of the students signed the principal's pledge. SNCC directed others to a local college that offered high school courses.

SNCC ended its voter registration drive in McComb in December, but only after it had stirred in the hearts and heads of Mississippi's black people the conviction that freedom, justice, and equality were worth the fight.

By the fall, when I returned to classes at UGA, court-ordered limited desegregation in Atlanta schools and elsewhere had begun. The massive white resistance, if not yet history, had been dealt a severe blow. There were more challenges to come, including more violence, an unresponsive federal government, and a long wait for full desegregation in Atlanta. But for now, Atlanta was working to live up to the description Mayor William B. Hartsfield had given it: "The City Too Busy to Hate."

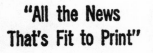

"All the News That's Fit to Print"

The New

VOL. CXII . No. 38,237.

© 1962 by The New York Times Company.
Times Square, New York 36, N. Y.

NEW YORK, TU

3,000 TROOPS PUT DOW
AND SEIZE 200 AS NEC
EX-GEN. WALKER IS H

SENATE REJECTS AID CUTS AND BAN ON HELP FOR REDS

Upholds Kennedy's Authority to Assist Nations That Do Business With Cuba

By FELIX BELAIR Jr.
Special to The New York Times.

WASHINGTON, Oct. 1—The Senate decided for the Administration today in preliminary votes on the foreign aid appropriation bill, due for passage tomorrow.

It voted, 47 to 28, against cutting $785,000,000 from the $792,400 000 of military and economic aid funds that its Appropriations Committee restored to the bill the House had cut heavily.

The effect of the vote was to hold the appropriation at $4,422,800,000, as recommended by its Appropriations Committee. The Administration had

Associated Press Wirep

PRISONERS ARE MARCHED TO ARMORY IN OXFORD: Army men escort a gro of prisoners to National Guard Armory. The group had participated in a disturbance was apprehended after the soldiers were ordered to fire at the feet of the riote

ork Times.

LATE CITY EDITION
U. S. Weather Bureau Report (Page 77) forecasts:
Mostly sunny today. Fair
tonight and tomorrow.
Temp. range: 75—54; yesterday: 74—52.

, OCTOBER 2, 1962.   10 cents beyond 50-mile zone from New York City
except on Long Island. Higher in air delivery cities.   FIVE CENTS

MISSISSIPPI RIOTING
RO ATTENDS CLASSES;
LD FOR INSURRECTION

SHOTS QUELL MOB

Enrolling of Meredith Ends Segregation in State Schools

By CLAUDE SITTON
Special to The New York Times

OXFORD, Miss., Oct. 1—
James H. Meredith, a Negro,
enrolled in the University of
Mississippi today and began
classes as Federal troops and
federalized units of the Mississippi National Guard quelled a
15-hour riot.

A force of more than 3,000
soldiers and guardsmen and 400
deputy United States marshals
fired rifles and hurled tear-gas
grenades to stop the violent
demonstrations.

Throughout the day more
troops streamed into Oxford.
Tonight a force approaching
5,000 soldiers and guardsmen,
along with the Federal marshals,
maintained an uneasy peace in
this town of 6,500 in the northern Mississippi hills.

[There were two flareups to-

United Press International Telephoto

ALKER IS STOPPED BY TROOPS: Former Maj. Gen. Edwin A. Walker is detained
soldiers near the courthouse in Oxford. He was turned over to U.S. marshals and is
ing held in $100,000 bail on charges stemming from his role in Sunday's campus riots.

1962

"Woke up this morning with my mind
stayed on freedom."
—*Freedom song*

In the fall of 1962, when quiet—if not racial harmony—had come to the University of Georgia, I was called to the telephone in the hallway outside my dormitory room.

"Hello Charlayne," an unfamiliar male voice on the other end began. "This is James."

"James who?" I asked.

"James Meredith," he responded.

James Meredith had just integrated Ole Miss, the University of Mississippi, so suspecting a racist prank, I immediately responded, "Prove it."

At this point, Meredith said, "Hold on and listen."

It was all too familiar. Into my ears rang the words that had welcomed me to the University of Georgia: "Two, four, six, eight. We don't wanna integrate."

Facing page: James H. Meredith was interviewed after registering at the University of Mississippi.

Previous pages: *The New York Times* front page from October 2, 1962. For full text of James Meredith article, see page 159.

And they were accompanied by the sound of firecrackers popping, or maybe in that volatile arena, bullets.

As hard as it was for me to hear that noise, I also had to smile as Meredith's voice returned to my ear.

"Convinced now?" he asked with about as much humor as I would ever hear from him.

Meredith was a military veteran and, at thirty, a bit older than the average student. But he had applied to Ole Miss the same month Hamp and I desegregated the University of Georgia—January 1961.

While the desegregation of Ole Miss would not enter history as the first, it was the most violent of the early efforts by blacks to crack what NAACP lawyers had long insisted was the most important wall to tear down—symbolically, as well as practically. For generations, state institutions like the University of Georgia had been home to the sons and daughters of white privilege, even though they were public, meaning they were supported by the taxes of blacks as well as whites. Those taxes went to create institutions that provided facilities that were much better than those at black colleges and universities.

Like our case in Georgia, Meredith's application for admission was repeatedly thwarted by various officials, including a federal court judge, who ruled that Meredith had failed to prove the university had a policy of denying admission to blacks. Eventually the case had reached the U.S. Supreme Court, which ruled that Meredith had the right to be admitted, but the governor of Mississippi refused to comply.

For political reasons, the Kennedy administration wanted to stay out of this fight. That is, the Kennedys did not want to offend their white Southern base of support or Southerners with powerful seniority positions in Congress. But as time went on, both Attorney General Robert F. Kennedy and the president were drawn into a behind-the-scenes drama involving repeated telephone calls between the Kennedys and Mississippi governor Ross Barnett. Threats were made on both sides—the Kennedys threatened to send soldiers, and at one point the governor proposed a "fake showdown" that would allow him to charge the federal

On September 29, 1962, while still blocking Meredith's admission to the University of Mississippi, Governor Ross Barnett waves a Confederate flag before the start of an Ole Miss football game.

government with "interposing" federal law on Mississippi. The Kennedys continued to tread carefully and even made concessions to the governor during four attempts by Meredith to register. Each time, Meredith was accompanied by two federal officials—Chief U.S. Marshal James McShane and the Justice Department's John Doar. On the first try, the governor himself acted as registrar and personally barred Meredith. In a televised address, he proclaimed: "No school in our state will be integrated while I am your governor. I shall do everything in my power to prevent integration in our schools."

Meredith's fight for admission, led by lawyers from the NAACP Legal Defense and Education Inc. Fund—Thurgood Marshall and Constance Baker Motley, who had also represented my case to attend UGA—lasted for a year, putting into stark relief the issue of state verses federal law in an atmosphere marked by intense racial explosions. Motley, the tall, handsome, no-nonsense legal trail-blazer, said that the Mississippi state officials' resistance to Meredith's application was their way of "playing out the last chapter of the Civil War," having "offered the most resistance since the Civil War to the idea of equality for blacks." The case lasted a year, but the lawyers were victorious, as Motley and her team kept to their chosen path, relying on the supremacy of federal over state law. Reflecting on the Ole Miss victory, Motley said the U.S. Constitution was "put to the test and survived."

Still, following the ruling, Governor Barnett created a series of obstacles in an attempt to prevent Meredith from enrolling.

Once again, the federal government was forced to act. Kennedy sent federal troops to escort Meredith on campus. When rioting broke out, federal officials were also in the line of fire, literally and figuratively. Governor Barnett stated that "federal authorities alone have the power to stop the bloodshed by re-moving Meredith and the thousand armed troops that are at his side." He also declared that there was "no case in history where the Caucasian race has sur-vived social integration." And he vowed, "We will not drink from the cup of genocide."

Two people died and scores were injured in the rioting, but neither the federal government nor Meredith withdrew. On October 2, 1962, James H. Mer-edith attended his first classes at Ole Miss.

By this time, the Kennedy administration was looking for ways to stop the stream of embarrassing news stories about violence in the South. It was a time when the U.S. government was engaged in a fight with the Soviet Union over which economic system would predominate in the world—American capitalism or Soviet communism. Along with Robert Kennedy, the president argued that there was little more to gain through the Freedom Rides and that the students would gain more from registering black voters. They also pledged to protect ac-tivists working to register voters and to help generate support. Although not all the activists were happy, especially SNCC's representatives, there was a consensus to put the focus on voting rights.

The president worked behind the scenes to encourage foundations to contribute to what came to be the Voter Education Project (VEP), and soon, with funds flowing into its coffers, the VEP, operating under the umbrella of an antiracist organization known as the Southern Regional Council, took on a life of its own. And despite concerns from SNCC and CORE members that voter registration was the weak sister of the civil rights movement and possibly a sneaky way to stop their direct action protests, Bob Moses got SNCC on board, and he and Dave Dennis of CORE became co-directors. Along with the NAACP's Medgar Evers,

On a voter registration drive, SNCC workers, led by Robert Moses (right), speak to a farm family in Mississippi.

they formed an organization that served as a coordinator and a dispenser of the voter project funds. It was called the Council of Federated Organizations, or COFO. The NAACP wasn't fond of SNCC and CORE, but Evers personally knew they had the shock troops to cover the vicious Mississippi terrain, and he was happy to join forces with them. Another NAACP leader, Aaron Henry, became the head of COFO, which set up headquarters in Greenwood, and began organizing demonstrations.

By the time Moses was joined by other activists and local people, the federal government was bringing lawsuits against county and state officials for voter intimidation. Mississippi's Laflore County board of supervisors struck back by withdrawing from the federal program that provided food to the poor. Once again, SNCC stepped up. SNCC's foot soldiers secured a truck and made as many as thirty trips to as far away as Michigan to collect food and medicine for the poor. After one of the long drives back to Clarksville, two activists, Ivanhoe Donaldson and Ben Taylor, arrived in town at 2:30 a.m. and found the drugstore, where they were supposed to drop their supplies, closed. So the two pulled over and went to sleep. Later, the police woke them up and threw them in jail, charged with transporting drugs across state lines. The drugs were aspirin for the poor. The NAACP's Inc. Fund came to their rescue and got them out of jail.

The food drive got national attention and the support of celebrities like comedian Dick Gregory, actor Sidney Poitier, and singer Harry Belafonte. All came to Greenwood in person to support the effort, and their presence helped dramatize the plight of poor Southern blacks.

During the fall and early winter of 1962, I only kept half an eye on the demonstrations happening outside of Georgia. Instead, I spent most of my time getting ready for graduation. This senior year was so different from my last year at Turner High School. Back then, I had been at the exciting center of almost everything, including attention. But attention was the last thing I wanted at the University of Georgia. I was a little bit worried that the whites who had so vehemently opposed my entry back in 1961 had only been laying low and that now they might choose graduation to take, like Custer, a last stand. Still, as I walked around the sprawling campus, admiring the beautiful green leaves turning to stunning orange and gold as they prepared their last display before winter, I went about making preparations for graduation. Like a normal senior, I took pictures for the yearbook and ordered invitations to send out for the graduation ceremony in June. I didn't want to leave out anybody who had helped me through these sometimes trying times. My mother had a great memory, so we were in constant contact about the list. In the end, it seemed as if I had invited half of Black Atlanta. And I suspected Hamp had invited the other half.

"All the News
at's Fit to Print"

The New

VOL. CXII . No. 38,568.
© 1963 by The New York Times Company.
Times Square, New York 36, N. Y.

NEW YORK, THU

ENNEDY SIGNS
LL AVERTING
RAIL STRIKE

EDENT IS SET

ation Imposed by gress—Vote in ouse 286-66

Kennedy's statement e found on Page 13.

OHN D. POMFRET
al to The New York Times

INGTON, Aug. 28 —
s passed today a bill
vented a national rail-
ike scheduled for mid-
esident Kennedy signed
iately.

ouse completed the Con-
al action. It adopted by
ng vote of 286 to 66
joint resolution passed
y by the Senate. The
provides for arbitration
wo principal issues in
oad work rules dispute
a strike for 180 days.
ction was without Fed-
edent. Never before in
ory of peacetime labor
has Congress imposed
n in a labor-manage-
pute.

8 Dead in Utah Mine;
Fate of 15 Unknown

Special to The New York Times

MOAB, Utah, Aug. 28 —
Eight men were known dead
today and 15 were trapped a
half-mile underground in a
potash mine rocked yesterday
by a severe explosion.

Two survivors hoisted to
the surface today reported
that three men were dead, at
least five were alive and the
fate of 15 was unknown.
Later, however, rescue workers deep in the mine spotted
five more bodies that officials
said might be the men whom
the survivors first believed
alive.

Rescuers were being ham-
pered by deadly gas, extreme
heat, water and mechanical
failures. A communications
breakdown added to their
frustrations.

Donald Hanna, 27 years old,
of Price and Paul McKinney,

Continued on Page 14, Column 3

U.S. SPURNS DENIAL
BY EM ON CRISIS

U.S. PRESSES U.N.
TO CONDEMN SYRIA
ON ISRAELI DEATHS

Stevenson Deplores Killing of Youths—Thant Assures Council on Cease-Fire

Text of Stevenson statement appears on Page 2.

By KATHLEEN TELTSCH
Special to The New York Times

UNITED NATIONS, N. Y.,
Aug. 28 — Adlai E. Stevenson
declared today that the recent
slaying of two Israeli farmers
by Syrians was "wanton murder" deserving the strongest
condemnation by the Security
Council.

The United States delegate,
followed by the British representative, gave forceful support
to Israel's charges arising from
the Aug. 20 ambush killing of
two 19-year-old Israelis at the
Almagor farm settlement.

Mr. Stevenson rejected Syria's
countercharges against Israel as
"not corroborated" by United
Nations investigations.

The United States policy
statement drew a favorable reaction from Michael S. Comay
of Israel, who said it encouraged
him to expect the Council to
take "firm and vigorous action."

Syrian Disapproves

However, there was disap-
proval from Dr. Salah el-Tarazi
of Syria, who criticized Mr.

200,00
IN OR
PRES

ork Times.

LATE CITY EDITI

U. S. Weather Bureau Report (Page 88) for
Cloudy with scattered showers to
partly cloudy tonight and tomor

Temp. range: 77—62; yesterday: 8
Temp.-Hum. Index: 70 to 75 / yesterday

, AUGUST 29, 1963.

TEN CEN

MARCH FOR CIVIL RIGHTS
ERLY WASHINGTON RALLY
DENT SEES GAIN FOR NEGR

ACTION ASKED N

10 Leaders of Pr
Urge Laws to E
Racial Inequit

*Excerpts from talks at
are printed on Page*

By E. W. KENWORT
Special to The New York Ti

WASHINGTON. Aug
More than 200,000 Am
most of them black bu
of them white, demon
here today for a full and
program of civil rights ar
job opportunities.

It was the greatest as
for a redress of grievanc
this capital has ever see

One hundred years a
days after Abraham Linc
joined the emancipated
to "abstain from all vi
and "labor faithfully for
able wages." this vast
proclaimed in march an
and through the speec
their leaders that they w

1963

... And before I'll be a slave
I'll be buried in my grave
And go home to my Lord
And be free.
—*Freedom song*

By the time spring rolled around in Georgia, I was starting to relax enough to think about how I would miss the smell of honeysuckle and the sight of landscapes adorned with white dogwood blossoms as I mentally prepared to move to New York. I had been to New York as a young girl and had seen green and leafy Central Park on the way uptown to Harlem. But my main recollection was of the asphalt streets we played hopscotch on, so I was starting to feel a little nostalgic about the parts of the South that I loved. The only dark clouds around were those created by the swarms of black starlings I often saw flying overhead as I walked to class.

While these same signs of spring were showing throughout the South, the activists working to change the political landscape had no time to enjoy them. Just one state away in Alabama, activists were figuring out ways to confront its wall of segregation. The Ku Klux Klan's Birmingham, Alabama, chapter not only

Facing page: Organizers of the March on Washington link hands to lead the crowd up the Mall to the Lincoln Memorial on August 28, 1963.

Previous pages: *The New York Times* front page from August 29, 1963. For full text of March article, see page 163.

was believed to be the most violent in the South, but it was tacitly supported by many in the police department and local government. It was here that the Klan attacked the Freedom Riders in 1961, unhindered by the police.

Local black activists like the Reverend Fred Shuttlesworth had been fighting to end segregation in Birmingham for over seven years and had suffered severe consequences, from both blacks and whites. Shuttlesworth's home had been bombed by segregationists, and some of them had also beaten him and stabbed his wife when they attempted to enroll their daughter in an all-white elementary school. After the NAACP was banned throughout the state following the Montgomery bus boycott, Shuttlesworth managed to organize the Alabama Christian Movement for Human Rights and later became a founding member of the SCLC. But there was so much vigilante violence that many blacks did not want to be seen with the black preacher. Others were opposed to what they thought were radical politics, preferring to talk with a newly elected white mayor who was supposed to be more liberal than his predecessor.

Shuttlesworth invited the SCLC to come to Birmingham, telling its leadership, "If you win in Birmingham, as Birmingham goes, so goes the nation." And Martin Luther King agreed that Birmingham would be the biggest and most important test of nonviolence. If it could work there, it could work anywhere. But the opposite was also on his mind. Coming fresh from what many, including the SCLC, regarded at the time as a failed campaign in Albany, the organization needed to restore its belief in itself and its principles. A failed campaign in Alabama could prove devastating.

The Birmingham project was called Project C. The *C* was for confrontation that would attract media attention and hopefully prick the conscience of the nation. Months prior to the launch, SCLC's Andrew Young, James Bevel, and Dorothy Cotton held out-of-state workshops for community leaders. They had learned from the Albany experience that demonstrators needed to be prepared in advance to respond to what they knew would be the inevitable violence of Birmingham's notoriously brutal sheriff, Bull Connor. (Should they need to spend time in the Birmingham jail they would need to be prepared with toothbrushes, washcloths, and warm clothing, which they had not had in Albany. They were also schooled in daily prayer, Bible study, and citizen education. They were determined to be ready.

On April 3, they believed they were. They launched an economic boycott of downtown businesses and issued the Birmingham Manifesto. It called for getting rid of the "whites only" water fountains and public toilets, and for desegregation of lunch counters. They also demanded that businesses and industry hire blacks, and that the charges against all citizens who had been arrested in nonviolent demonstrations be dropped. And finally, they called for a biracial committee to work out plans for even broader desegregation. But while the SCLC's representatives met with a delegation of white business and religious leaders, little pressure resulted from the demonstrations, which were joined by only a few blacks and were otherwise largely ignored.

On Good Friday, April 16, Martin Luther King, Jr., uncharacteristically dressed in blue jeans and a blue cotton shirt, began a fifteen-minute walk to Birmingham's downtown. The aim of the march was to dramatize the need for an Easter boycott of downtown white stores that had no black employees, but whose sales rose each year when blacks shopped for their clothes to wear to church on Easter Sunday. That's why Dr. King and his aides were wearing jeans. The march swelled to a thousand blacks and one white man. The march would pass by Kelley Ingram Park, which was in the black neighborhood, and word had spread throughout the community that Dr. King himself would be leading the march. So there were many curious onlookers. But no sooner had they passed the park than the marchers collided with a massive police presence. The police had set up barricades to prevent the marchers from reaching downtown, and they wasted no time storming into the marchers, roughly pushing into the paddy wagon Dr. King and his top aides, the Rev. Ralph Abernathy, Fred Shuttlesworth, and Wyatt Walker. The police wielded batons and unleashed their dogs into the rest of the demonstrators.

Andrew Young, said they had never before witnessed such abuse by the police, as if they were "spoiling for a fight." One hundred and five people were arrested.

The rest made it back to the Sixteenth Street Baptist Church, where some were so angry they were calling for retaliation, something the SCLC definitely didn't want. Young tried to calm the crowd with his words, but what did calm the people was a song the SCLC's Dorothy Cotton began singing:

> Oh Freedom. Oh Freedom.
> Oh Freedom over me.
> And before I'll be a slave
> I'll be buried in my grave
> And go home to my Lord
> And be free.

Cotton's singing and Young's words saved the day for nonviolence and renewed the determination to fight the racist system. They all left the church singing what was essentially the anthem of the civil rights movement: "Ain't gonna let nobody turn me 'roun'."

IT WAS WHILE DR. KING was in jail that a group of white clergymen published an open letter arguing that the best way to resolve the issue of racial discrimination was not in the streets, but in the courts. Dr. King's legal representatives took him a copy of the letter, and soon he was busy crafting a response. The Gandhian nonviolent approach regarded negotiation as being as important as demonstrations, but when people negotiated in bad faith, Dr. King asserted, then it was necessary to move on to the next step. Dr. King's response was contained in his "Letter from a Birmingham Jail," written in the margins of newspapers one of the black jailhouse workers had smuggled to him and on a legal pad his lawyers had brought into his cell. In the letter, Dr. King argued against the admonition to go slow in a city that was, in his words, "probably the most thoroughly segregated city in the United States." He went on to talk about the city's widely known "ugly record of brutality," and the "grossly unjust treatment in the courts" he and many other blacks experienced. And he then pointed out there had been more "unsolved bombings of Negro homes and churches in Birmingham than in any other city in the nation." What Dr. King did not say was that there had been so many bombings that the city had been nicknamed "Bombingham."

Patiently and in great detail, Dr. King talked about the duplicity of white leaders, their call for blacks to wait, which he wrote, "always meant 'never,'" and concluded that direct action was now needed because the community had refused to negotiate. And he argued that direct action was also needed "to create a situation so crisis packed that it will inevitably open the door to negotiation." At the same time, Dr. King didn't let black people off the hook. He criticized complacency born of years of oppression, as well as those who "profit by segregation," and thus had become "insensitive to the problems of the masses."

Dr. Martin Luther King and the Reverend Ralph Abernathy were arrested by the Birmingham police for leading a march urging an Easter boycott of white stores that had no black employees.

Dr. King also warned of the possibility that frustration would lead blacks into more radical Black Nationalism. Yet, he held out hope that the pioneering struggles of "the real heroes," the "disinherited children of God" who had broken down the racial barriers in nonviolent protests, those who were "in reality standing up for the American dream and for the most sacred values of our Judeo-Christian heritage," would bring the nation back to the "great wells of democracy which were dug deep by the founding fathers in their formulation of the Constitution and the Declaration of Independence."

A few days later, despite the reluctance of the older movement activists to allow teenagers to protest, the "disinherited" black teenagers took to the streets.

The SCLC had trained them both in the techniques of nonviolent protest and the Gandhian philosophy behind it.

James Bevel, an SCLC lieutenant, had given the lecture "The Water Tower of Segregation." As top King aide Andrew Young recalled, "Bevel reminded us that segregation could not last without psychological assistance from blacks themselves and a lack of faith in our own heritage and potential."

Young was among those worried about the "ethics of taking teenage demonstrators out of school." But he reasoned that segregation had "poisoned their lives" and "restricted the possibilities of their futures." Initially, the group insisted that participants be older than fourteen, but younger kids came anyway, many—some as young as six—to be with their older siblings. All had to sign pledges that they would be nonviolent.

Bull Connor, the white sheriff of Birmingham, was having none of it. He sent his firemen, and they opened hard-hitting water hoses on the demonstrators, the force so great it knocked many of them down. The policemen continued their waterborne assault, which sent many of the children rolling down the street. And then Connor ordered his policemen to unleash their vicious dogs. But the youngsters in the two-day "Children's Crusade" kept marching, leading Young to later write, "Some have commented that the drenching of blacks in Birmingham by the fire hoses was an act of baptism in the new movement for human freedom."

That movement led to negotiations and then produced a settlement with the white power structure of Birmingham.

Meanwhile, Hamp continued his mostly solitary campus life, going to class and retreating to the black community, where he let off steam and bore the isolation by playing basketball with some of the young black boys from the neighborhood. When we first enrolled at Georgia, he had wanted to play football, but the university officials said no, fearing that either his own white teammates or those from other schools not yet desegregated might hurt him on purpose. So instead of excelling on the football field, he did so in his studies, generally scoring much higher than his classmates on any test they were given. He and I were frequently asked to speak outside of Athens. Black people were eager to share our experience by sharing our stories. He was the better student, but I was the better speaker and did more than Hamp. By the time the spring of our senior year had arrived, I was tired and just wanted to finish those last few weeks getting ready to graduate. But when Vernon Jordan asked me to speak one last time at an NAACP fund-raiser in Tampa, Florida, I agreed, in part so that I could see my father, who had retired from the army and was pastoring a church there. When I got to Tampa, I finally met James Meredith in person. There was a large crowd at the church, and I stood before them and shared our story, telling them at the end that we would soon graduate and how much support like theirs had helped us through. When I finished, I was exhausted until the people in the audience erupted in thunderous applause. They were still living under the heavy cloak of racism. But I could see when the evening was over that even my little speech about our experiences had given them some hope and perhaps even the courage

On orders from Sheriff Bull Connor, the Birmingham police broke up a demonstration by Birmingham teenagers using attack dogs and fire hoses on May 3, 1963. Photos like these outraged people in the rest of the country and helped draw attention to the need for equal rights.

to combat the racism that was keeping them down in Tampa and throughout Florida. Although I was weary, when so many people of all ages came up to me expressing such gratitude for what Hamp and I had done, I perked up immediately and was inspired all over again to "keep on keepin' on."

Back at UGA, Hamilton was soon to learn that his almost perfect grades had resulted in his being elected to Phi Beta Kappa, the country's highest academic honor society, as well as Phi Kappa Phi, another honor society for the highest academic achievers.

On that warm June 1 morning, as I prepared to head to the hall where graduates were to put on their long black robes, I was still a bit uneasy. Not only was I concerned about some student saying or doing something that would recall those ugly early days at the university, but civil rights demonstrations were still going on throughout the South, and the graduation speaker was arch-segregationist Richard B. Russell. I was a bit worried about potentially provocative words from him. But I managed to get over my anxieties and robed up, along with hundreds of other sons and daughters of Georgia.

Meanwhile, Alabama was getting its second challenge to its segregated state university. The first effort by Autherine Lucy had been short-lived. In 1953, Lucy had already graduated from an all-black college, but she wanted to study for an advanced degree in library science. Since the University of Alabama was segregated, Lucy enlisted the help of NAACP lawyers Thurgood Marshall, Arthur Shoors, and the woman who would become one of the lead lawyers in my case six years later, Constance Baker Motley. The trio won a court order directing the university to admit Lucy, and the university complied, although it barred her from the dining hall and the dormitories. Three days after her admission on February 3, 1956, a student riot broke out and Lucy was suspended, allegedly "for her own safety." Again, the NAACP lawyers went to court to oppose the action, but the university officials prevailed. Marshall called the reasons for Lucy's expulsion

Facing page: Hamilton Holmes and I embrace, celebrating our graduation from an institution where we had been able to pursue our dreams like all other sons and daughters of Georgia.

"a cunning stratagem," suggesting that the university officials and the rioters conspired together. And that provided the university with the pretext for expelling Lucy permanently. It argued that Lucy had slandered the university and therefore had no place inside its classrooms. Marshall later admitted he had used a poor choice of words. But that chapter had ended and another would not be written until 1963.

That year, on June 10, in an exercise in dramatics that made news around the world, Governor George C. Wallace kept a campaign promise by attempting to stop desegregation at "the schoolhouse door." A lectern had been placed at the door of the auditorium where Vivian Malone and James Hood, two black twenty-year-olds, were due to register. Despite sweltering heat that had already reached 100 degrees in mid-morning, the governor wore a suit and tie, along with a stern look. He stood at the lectern as he read his prepared statement. Malone and Hood waited in the nearby car of Nicholas Katzenbach, deputy attorney general of the United States and, by this time, a veteran of various civil rights challenges.

"The unwelcomed, unwanted, unwarranted and force-induced intrusion upon the campus of the University of Alabama today of the might of the Central Government offers a frightful example of the oppression of the rights, privileges and sovereignty of this state by officers of the Federal Government," Wallace defiantly intoned. He went on to talk about the Tenth Amendment, which provides that powers not delegated to the federal government are retained by the states. "I stand here today, as Governor of this sovereign state, and refuse to willingly submit to illegal usurpation of power by the Central Government," Wallace declared.

As a *Times* correspondent, Claude Sitton wrote: "The Governor implied that there might have been violence were it not for his presence when he said: 'I stand before you today in place of thousands of other Alabamians whose presence would have confronted you had I been derelict and neglected to fulfill the responsibilities of my office.'"

Sitton continued:

> He concluded by asserting that he did "denounce and forbid this illegal and unwarranted action by the Central Government."

"I take it from that statement that you are going to stand in the door and that you are not going to carry out the orders of the court," said Mr. Katzenbach, "and that you are going to resist us from doing so. Is that correct?"

"I stand according to my statement," replied Mr. Wallace.

"Governor, I am not interested in a show," Mr. Katzenbach went on. "I don't know what the purpose of this show is. I am interested in the orders of these courts being enforced."

The federal official then told the governor that the latter had no choice but to comply.

In the end, it may all have been a show, as it appears that Wallace had made a deal with the federal government that he would take a stand on principle, to save face, but that it would be brief. And it was indeed to be Wallace's last stand against school desegregation. On that day, Katzenbach told the governor: "From the outset, Governor, all of us have known that the final chapter of this history will be the admission of these students."

As preoccupied as I was with ending one chapter of my life and beginning another, I couldn't help but look at young Vivian Malone as a sister in the struggle, not least because she even looked like she could have been my real sister, tall and honey-colored, with a short, bouffant hairdo popular at the time. When I saw pictures of her in class, surrounded by hostile whites, I knew what effort that took and could almost read her mind as I looked at her staring straight ahead. I could see the look of determination in her eyes—that she would do whatever it took to keep those eyes on her prize. Still, the pressures remained, and James Hood left after two months, citing "a complete mental and physical breakdown." But despite bomb threats and actual bombs being set off four blocks from her dormitory, Malone stayed the course, often smiling at white students who ignored her. I also knew what effort that took because I had been there.

My summer was a happy one. I had married the white Southern student I met at UGA who spoke French like a Frenchman. The interracial marriage was the segregationists' worst nightmare, as many insisted integration of their institutions would lead to race mixing, which they equated with "mongrelization." I spent the few weeks after graduation getting ready to move to New York and start new chapters in my life.

But it was not a happy summer for Mississippi. The state was the poorest in the nation, with some three-quarters of the state's black population living below the poverty line. Not only were they economically poor, they were also politically poor. Few black people in Mississippi were allowed to vote or participate in any way in the decisions that affected their lives. And in the summer of 1963, there was a lot of violence aimed at keeping things just the way they always had been. Since SNCC had come in to help change that, a lot of the violence was directed at their workers. That summer, Jimmy Travis, a local SNCC worker, was shot in the head and shoulder by passing whites. Travis survived and so did the movement. Yet, Medgar Evers didn't. The head office of the NAACP continued to keep its distance from SNCC shock troops—except to represent them in court or to bail them out of jail—but Evers embraced SNCC. Evers threw himself into the voter registration drive with a passion, living a life "never knowing when that bullet was going to hit," as his wife Myrlie once recalled. She and their young family had received death threats, and they had already survived the bombing of their house. Their three children—nine-year-old Darrell, eight-year-old Reena, and three-year-old Vann—had been taught to dive to the floor even at the sound of a car backfiring.

Evers had survived World War II, but he didn't survive the battle for freedom back home. On June 12, 1963, his family was watching John F. Kennedy deliver his strongest statement yet on civil rights. Kennedy complimented officials at the University of Alabama for admitting Malone and Hood. Just as he had in Mississippi, Kennedy had federalized the Alabama National Guard to help make the University of Alabama's integration peaceful and had stood down the defiant governor. In his June 12 address, the president reminded viewers of the nation's founding principle—"that all men are created equal"—and insisted that "the rights of every man are diminished when the rights of one are threatened." As the speech was playing on a set inside his house, Medgar Evers was shot in his driveway. He died at his front door. He was thirty-eight years old.

Even on the day of his funeral, the police segregated the mourners—making black marchers walk on a separate street designated for blacks. And that was more than some of the marchers could take. On that day, it became clear that not every black person had signed on to non-violence, so tired were they of being sick and tired, as an old movement saying went. Many of the black mourners came close to rioting. To make matters worse, there was no justice at the time for Evers's murder. The man who shot him, Byron De La Beckwith, had been arrested, but an all-white jury would soon acquit him of the murder.

These horrible racial realities only served to fuel the fire of the simmering rage in black communities all over the country. From Harlem, New York, to Savannah, Georgia, black anger spilled over into the streets, some less peaceful than others. More than 900 demonstrators marched or staged sit-ins and otherwise protested in more than a hundred cities. More than 20,000 were arrested, and there were at least ten deaths.

All of this made the Kennedys extremely nervous. The global battle with the Soviet Union was still being waged, and bad international publicity was not

Myrlie Evers, Medgar Evers's widow, comforted her son Darrell during the slain civil rights leader's funeral in Jackson, Mississippi, June 1963.

helping their cause. While the Kennedys had been quietly working to raise funds in support of voting rights campaigns, the civil rights leadership was raising funds for a frontal assault on segregation, a march on the nation's capital by thousands. The still-wary Kennedys tried in vain to get them to call it off.

But on August 28, 1963, the movement took its cause to the nation's capitol and to the American people. I was sitting in the office of *The New Yorker* magazine in New York City, having been hired just after graduation by the legendary editor William Shawn. I was working as an editorial assistant, typing rejection letters to would-be writers and doing other office chores. In my spare time, I worked on articles I hoped to get in the magazine. My dream of becoming a journalist was coming true. But the doors were still closed to most young black people with dreams, which is why I sat glued to the television screen with tears running down my cheeks on the day that Martin Luther King spoke with moving eloquence about his dream.

The Rev. Fred Shuttlesworth tried to register two black boys in a Birmingham, Alabama, elementary school but was turned away by state troopers.

It was on this hot August day that a coalition of civil rights organizations, including SNCC, pulled off the biggest public demonstration for civil rights in the country's history. It was held on the grassy mall that spreads out under the stone-cast gaze of the president known as the Great Emancipator, Abraham Lincoln. At that time, black unemployment was at least twice that of whites, and full freedom that included the right to vote was still denied to the majority of blacks in the South. The civil rights movement's goals had been broadened to include economic justice as one of the most basic promises of equality, and the event was billed as a march "for jobs and freedom."

In addition to the leaders and officials of the various civil rights organizations, thousands of ordinary black people had journeyed from the South's big towns and rural areas. They were joined by blacks from other parts of the country and many white supporters—all of whom that day "voted with their feet," as march organizer Bayard Rustin put it.

Nervous federal officials worried that so many black people in one place might result in a riot and called out some 4,000 troops, and 15,000 paratroopers stood by in North Carolina. Liquor sales were banned for the first time since Prohibition.

Speakers included prominent figures from the movement, including James Farmer and John Lewis, but with his "I Have a Dream" speech, Martin Luther King, Jr., owned the day, giving what became the signature scripture of the March on Washington.

Many remember the speech for its hopefulness, found in King's rhythmic repetition of his dream. But it was a speech that was as much an indictment of the status quo as it was a message of hope. It was a speech that foretold the gradual shift from civil rights to economic justice. Dr. King began:

Five score years ago, a great American, in whose symbolic shadow we stand today, signed the Emancipation Proclamation. This momentous decree came as a great beacon light of hope to millions of Negro slaves who had been seared in the flames of withering injustice. It came as a joyous daybreak to end the long night of their captivity.

But one hundred years later, the Negro still is not free. One hundred years later, the life of the Negro is still sadly crippled by the manacles of segregation and the chains of discrimination. One hundred years later, the Negro lives on a lonely island of poverty in the midst of a vast ocean of

Dr. Martin Luther King gives his "I Have a Dream" speech to the many thousands of people gathered on the Mall for the March on Washington, August 28.

material prosperity. One hundred years later, the Negro is still languishing in the corners of American society and finds himself an exile in his own land. So we have come here today to dramatize a shameful condition.

Even if it looked like a scene out of a huge picnic, hardly anyone spoke, so heavy was the air with Dr. King's powerful metaphors. He said the group had come to "cash a check," and then explained:

When the architects of our republic wrote the magnificent words of the Constitution and the Declaration of Independence, they were signing a promissory note to which every American was to fall heir. This note was a promise that all men, yes, black men as well as white men, would be guaranteed the unalienable rights of life, liberty, and the pursuit of happiness.

It is obvious today that America has defaulted on this promissory note insofar as her citizens of color are concerned.

Dr. King reiterated the message of nonviolence, insisting that the struggle must be conducted "on the high plane of dignity and discipline."

And then, Dr. King built toward his soaring climax with the rhythmic cadence he was famous for, the theme of his speech, "I have a dream."

> Let freedom ring . . . From every mountainside, let freedom ring. And when this happens, when we allow freedom to ring, when we let it ring from every village and every hamlet, from every state and every city, we will be able to speed up that day when all of God's children, black men and white men, Jews and Gentiles, Protestants and Catholics, will be able to join hands and sing in the words of the old Negro spiritual, "Free at last! Free at last! Thank God Almighty, we are free at last!"

And indeed, Dr. King lifted the spirits of all those who had gathered on the mall, and soon eased the earlier fears of those concerned about violence and disruption. The marchers left as they had come, determined but nonviolent. And a clean-up crew from the coalition picked up every scrap of paper left on the mall.

In an unprecedented step, all three television networks broadcast the speech live. I watched it sitting behind my desk with many of my *New Yorker* colleagues. Three years earlier, I had been prevented from joining in the sit-ins because of my pending case against the state of Georgia, but I had managed to make a contribution to the overall struggle for justice and equality. Now, as a journalist, I was in a similar boat. I could not be an activist *and* a journalist. That would amount to a conflict of interest. But I could still make a contribution by reporting on people who had been excluded from the white-controlled media. I resolved to seek out stories that showed black people in all their humanity—their problems, as well as their achievements, their struggles as well as their victories.

I wasn't, by a long shot, the only one watching the march that day. In addition to millions of others across the globe, President John F. Kennedy also watched. He later met with the leaders of the march and told them, "One cannot help but be impressed with the deep fervor and quiet dignity that characterizes the thousands who have gathered in the nation's capital from across the country to demonstrate their faith and confidence in our form of government."

Earlier in the day, in a Labor Day statement, Kennedy had told the officials there that the government had to "accelerate its efforts to achieve equal rights for all our citizens—in employment, in education and in all sectors of our national activity."

Still, the goal of the marchers was to force passage of the Civil Rights Act, calling for an end to discrimination on the basis of gender as well as race in hiring, promoting, and firing. And despite Kennedy's lofty words, the venerable old leader of the march, seventy-four-year-old A. Philip Randolph, nevertheless aligned himself with radicals like those in SNCC when he pressed for continuing demonstrations, arguing that it was only pressure that moved senators and congressmen.

This was certainly true of the South, especially in Birmingham. Whites all over the South were reeling after the courts ordered school desegregation. But eighteen days after the triumphant March on Washington, it became clear the positive international response to the event didn't have much impact among the white supremacists in Alabama. Already there had been two bombs set off in black areas of Birmingham. And now, a third was about to explode.

Sunday, September 15, was Youth Day at the Sixteenth Street Baptist Church in Birmingham. Children were all dressed in white for their duties during the church service. But they never got to perform them. A bomb made of fifteen sticks of dynamite exploded in the church, tearing four of the young girls to pieces. Denise McNair, at eleven, was the youngest. Her parents identified her at the morgue by her feet and the ring on her finger. The other children killed were Addie May Collins, Carole Robertson, and Cynthia Wesley, all fourteen years old.

Some whites joined the black community in mourning. Eight thousand people attended the funeral, including some white clergy. But the prevailing white sentiment was reflected in the fact that the FBI knew who had committed the crime but would remain silent. That same day, a thirteen-year-old black boy riding on the handlebars of his friend's bicycle was murdered by a couple of Eagle Scouts.

Once again, despite exhortations to nonviolence, the anger in the black community could not be contained. Many young blacks took to the streets, hurling rocks at white youth. The police did not just shoot to break up the demonstrations, they shot to kill. One of their victims was shot in the back of the head, indicating that he was fleeing police when he was killed.

Martin Luther King was also angry over the events and, once again, not only at the vicious whites. "What murdered these four girls?" he asked in a press conference, then went on to answer: "The apathy and complacency of many Negroes who will sit down on their stools and do nothing and not engage in creative protest to get rid of this evil."

In Mississippi, on Election Day in November, blacks who had not been allowed to vote in the Democratic primary in June staged their own election. With an integrated slate, they held what they called a "Freedom Vote" to demonstrate their deep desire to vote. Some 80,000 black Mississippians cast their ballots and laid the foundation for an integrated party that would soon challenge the all-white Mississippi Democratic Party.

By this time, the civil rights movement was making its biggest splashes ever on national and international news, which was a key element in the movement's strategy. They believed such pressure would help force the Kennedy administration to do even more to protect the activists. But in just three more months, on November 22, 1963, John F. Kennedy was murdered in Dallas, Texas. He never got to sign his civil rights bill.

TURKISH PREMIER AT WHITE HOUSE: Ismet Inonu is welcomed by Presiden Johnson on arrival by helicopter from Williamsburg, Va., where he spent Sunday nigh

of Turkey reviewed crisis at two meet- as political forces pressed the Premier y United States ef- npromise.

men met for 50 min- orning at the White nediately after the ader, his wife and rived from Williams- He had spent the following his flight ra.

lso discussed the blem at a luncheon Mr. Johnson. Later ed a reception at the nbassy.

h-ranking Cyprus nt official confirmed George Grivas, for- r of Greek Cypriote against the British, Cyprus. A Greek nt spokesman said l's purpose was to ote peace.]

See Rusk and Ball

son and Mr. Inonu final conference to- ternoon, but impor- ntive discussions are take place in the State Depart- re the 79-year-old d his advisers will Secretary of State and Under Secretary Ball.

n purpose of United macy is to persuade y and Greece to re- any actions that d to a war over the same time, the s seeking to lead the nments to agree to irectly on the future terranean island. ere no indications to- Mr. Inonu's reaction Johnson's attempt on.

rmal remarks on ar- Premier told the

eve in peace, but we that peace cannot unless it is based on

nd phase of the Presi-

U.S. Confident That Reds Grasp Warnings on Asia

By JACK RAYMOND
Special to The New York Times

WASHINGTON, June 22—The State Department said today there could be little doubt that Communist leaders throughout the world fully understood that the United States was determined to repel aggression in Southeast Asia.

A brief statement, read by a department spokesman, Richard I. Phillips, was designed to assure those who feared "another Korea" that the United States was making its warning messages understood.

Many persons believe that the Korean war would not have broken out if the Communists had been adequately warned of United States intentions to defend South Korea. Today's statement, in answer to a question on the possibility of a major war in Asia, was based on recent diplomatic moves as well as military and public relations actions.

De Gaulle Warning Assumed

It is assumed here, for example, that President de Gaulle relayed to the Chinese Communist Ambassador in Paris, whom he saw last week, a warning of the United States attitude that was conveyed to him by Under Secretary of State George W. Ball.

In addition, it is understood that the British Government has relayed similar warnings through its embassy in Peking.

These diplomatic moves coincided with United States military reconnaissance flights over Laos and public statements by high American officers.

BRITISH ARMS AID IN INDOCHINA SEEN

Show of Support for U.S. Is Expected—Bolstering of Malaysia Also Due

By LAWRENCE FELLOWS
Special to The New York Times

LONDON, June 22 — Britain can be expected to make soon a show of military support for the United States in Indochina, it was reliably reported tonight.

One qualified source said the support would probably be similar to that extended in 1962. At that time the United States sent marines and the Royal Air Force dispatched a squadron to Thailand to counter a Communist threat.

The British will also strengthen, with additional helicopters and other equipment, their own military forces battling Indonesian guerrillas on the Malaysian frontier, it was learned.

Separate Treatment

The Malaysia issue, however, was being treated here as a separate problem and one of much smaller dimensions.

CLEANERS AT FAI DEFEND SERVICE

Allied and Moses Aides Te Rates Proper and Decla Quality of Work Is Goo

By WALTER CARLSON

The World's Fair and the lied Maintenance Corporat the principal subcontractor the fairgrounds, defended y terday the rates and the qua of the housekeeping serv performed for the exhibito

Allied Maintenance has c under increasing criticism f exhibitors, angered by w they consider high costs poor maintenance. As a res the fair is facing formal c plaints from some exhibitor

Even as a defense was b voiced, new complaints w being registered by pavi managers. And the exhibi in general expressed gratif tion that "the situation was nally coming to a head."

Statements by fair offic and Allied were directed at article that appeared in New York Times yesterday which exhibitors' compla were quoted. The compla will be aired further tomor at a meeting with a fair resentative.

Statement by Moses

Robert Moses, president the fair corporation, issue statement on the compla and criticized what he ter "a broadside attack on u practices and maintenance

lems peculiar to an urban
[ver]sity.

r. James M. Hester, presi-
of the university, said the
[i]t was made to help N.Y.U.
[i] "a great metropolitan uni-
[i]ty of the future and to
[dem]onstrate how teaching and
[rese]arch in the city can be
[b]e most effective."

[Th]e long-range program calls
[for] far more rigid academic
[stan]dards and more facilities
[for r]esident undergraduate and
[grad]uate students.

More Housing Planned

[Dr]. Hester said in an inter-
[view] that the ultimate aim was
[to h]ouse at least 25 per cent
[of th]e students at the uni-
[versi]ty's Washington Square
[cam]pus in dormitories and uni-
[vers]ity-owned apartments, com-
[pare]d with fewer than 10 per
[cent] now.

["C]ritical priority will be
[give]n to the construction of a
[new] library," Dr. Hester said.
["Th]is is not to be just a
[grea]t university library," he
[said], "but rather a place where
[stud]ents and faculty can work
[and] study and around which an
[acad]emic community can be
[buil]t."

[Th]e library and study cen-
[ter,] which will be next to the
[Loeb] Student Center on the
[nort]h side of Washington
[Squ]are, will have a capacity of
[one] million volumes and
[seat]ing accommodations for
[mor]e than 3,000 persons.

Fund Drive in Offing

[Dr]. Hester said it was im-
[port]ant that "going to an urban
[univ]ersity does not seem like
[goin]g to high school," and de-
[scri]bed the over-all goal as one
[of] making N.Y.U. "a place for
[New] Yorkers and a place for
[peo]ple who want to come to
[New] York."

[T]he $75 million in additional
[fun]ds must be raised from non-
[gov]ernmental sources over five
[yea]rs. Dr. Hester said a fund-
[rais]ing drive was being planned.
[Howe]ver, the foundation will
[adva]nce an initial $4 million to
[the] university at once, before
[the] money is raised under the

Justice Douglas wrote one of
his own as well as joining
Justice Goldberg's.

The dissent was by Justice
Tom C. Clark. It was joined
by Justices John Marshall Harlan and Byron R. White.

USE OF CONFESSION IN TRIAL IS CURBED

Court Bars It as Evidence if Suspect Can't See Lawyer or Is Not Told of Rights

Special to The New York Times
WASHINGTON, June 22 —
A 5-to-4 majority of the Supreme Court placed a sharp
new restriction today on the
use of confessions in criminal
trials.

If the police focus on a principal suspect, the Court said,
and question him without let-
ting him see his lawyers or
without warning him that his
answers may be used against
him, any resulting confession
must be barred from evidence.

Justice Arthur J. Goldberg
wrote the decision, which is
likely to have broad effects on
law enforcement across the
country. The ruling was based
on the integrity of the right
to counsel—a right applied in
full force just last year to state
as well as to Federal trials.

A strong dissent by Justice
Byron R. White was joined by
Justices Tom C. Clark and
Potter Stewart. Justice John
Marshall Harlan dissented sep-
arately, and Justice Stewart
also wrote his own dissenting
opinion.

"I do not suggest for a moment that law enforcement will
be destroyed by the rule announced today," Justice White
said. "The need for peace and
order is too insistent for that.

"But it will be crippled and
its task made a great deal

---

3 IN RIGHTS DRIVE REPORTED MISSING

Mississippi Campaign Heads Fear Foul Play—Inquiry by F.B.I. Is Ordered

By CLAUDE SITTON
Special to The New York Times
PHILADELPHIA, Miss., June
22—Three workers in a day-
old civil rights campaign in
Mississippi were reported missing today after their release
from jail here last night.

Leaders of the drive said they
feared that the three men—two
whites, both from New York,
and one Negro—had met with
foul play.

The three had been held by
Neshoba County authorities for
four hours following the arrest
of one on a speeding charge
and the jailing of the others
"for investigation."

Agents of the Federal Bureau
of Investigation began arriving
here in force early tonight after
the Justice Department ordered
a full-scale search.

The Mississippi Highway Patrol issued a missing-persons
bulletin, but a spokesman in
Jackson indicated late today
that it had no plans at present
for further action.

All three missing men ar-
rived in Mississippi late Saturday afternoon from Oxford,
Ohio, where they had taken
part in a one-week orientation
course for the statewide project. They were among the advance group of some 175 workers who are expected to be

---

[a p]rohibition on Government
employment.

In 1961 the Supreme Court
upheld a finding that the Communist party must register under the act. But the Court did

Continued on Page 17, Column 1

Court reversed today
[con]victions of 42 sit-in d[emonstra]-
tors, but without rea[ching a]
fundamental constitu[tional is]-
sue involved.

The issue is whethe[r the Con]-
stitution itself, witho[ut affirma]-
tive action by Cong[ress, pro]-
hibits the states from [enforc]-
ing for trespass pe[ople who]
demand service with[out regard to]
discrimination at [privately]
owned places of busi[ness.]

Six Justices did [not rule]
on that question, and [they]
divided down the mid[dle. Three]
said the Constitution [does]
apply, and three sa[id it did not.]
did.

Varying majoritie[s were used,]
however, in reversin[g the]
convictions from [Florida,]
South Carolina and F[lorida]
decisions went o[n narrow]
grounds.

Congress Is A[ffected]

The result is to [return the]
basic issue to Congr[ess, which]
is just now resolvin[g the]
civil rights bill expe[cted to]
come law soon wi[th its ban on]
segregation in [restaurants,]
hotels, theaters and o[ther places]
of amusement.

Passage of the b[ill]
will dispose of the g[reat prob]-
lem of discriminatio[n. But re]-
maining for the cou[rts to set]-
tle will be the the [issue of the]
sit-in convictions alr[eady pend]-
ing, which will not [be affected]
by the new statute.

Having wrestled [inconclu]-
sively with the const[itutionality]
of these convictions, [the Court]
agreed today to try [again next]
term. It agreed to [hear five]
more sit-in cases, f[rom North]
Carolina and Arkan[sas.]

Today was the l[ast day of]
the present term, a[nd it was]
an unusually busy on[e. The Jus]-
tices read opinions r[unning]
162 pages of opini[on in the]
sit-in cases alone.

Line-Up Com[pared]

The line-up on th[is issue in]
the sit-in cases was o[dd.]

Justices Arthur [Goldberg]
and William O. Do[uglas]

HUMAN RIGHTS
“No American can
rest while any American
is denied his rights....”
FREE
MISS.

1964

This little light of mine, I'm gonna let it shine,
Let it shine, let it shine, let it shine.
—*Old Negro spiritual sung by civil rights activists*

During the summer of '64, white and black students from Northern states poured into Mississippi to join what they believed was a righteous crusade—to register to vote as many black Mississippians as possible. It was known as Freedom Summer. Tom Hayden was a member of the Northern-based, white-led activist organization Students for a Democratic Society and served as a liaison between it and SNCC. He believed that if white official violence only targeted black sharecroppers and civil rights workers, then the rest of the country, which was "significantly prejudiced," would not become engaged with the struggle for civil rights. In order to achieve the goals of the movement, Hayden reasoned "it would be necessary to bring down the white sons and daughters of the country's middle class from the liberal North . . . to experience the true nature of southern segregation."

But for the young Northerners, the youthful SNCC workers were the draw. Admired for their courage and commitment, the men and women of SNCC had

Facing page: On August 24, 1964, Fannie Lou Hamer entered the Democratic National Convention Hall in Atlantic City.

Previous pages: *The New York Times* front page from June 23, 1964. For full text of rights drive article, see page 167.

achieved an almost mythical status in the eyes of the Northern students. And so, the students eagerly answered the call from SNCC, which had flooded college campuses in the North with a prospectus that called for "a nationwide mobilization." It was aimed at soliciting "a massive participation of Americans dedicated to the elimination of racial oppression."

Some SNCC members worried about the morality of sending white students into such a volatile atmosphere, where they would be seen as traitors to their race and might be beaten or even killed. But in the end, the decision was made to go forward with their participation. Jonathan Stein, a white college senior coordinating his campus recruitment, explained his motivation for going: "I think college students have a debt which they owe to society, and I think this is one way that college students can make a contribution for the four years of education they have had."

Peter Orris, who had grown up in New York City, was seventeen when he met SNCC workers at the March on Washington. When he was a college freshman, he attended one of SNCC's regional meetings in Atlanta. He saw SNCC as being involved in a "movement for racial justice" and wanted to be a part of it. So did other white students from Ivy League universities like Harvard and Yale. They were, in some ways, like the young people who got involved in the U.S. presidential campaign of 2008. In both cases, the young people were moved by idealism and the desire to be involved in something that would make a difference in people's lives. And in both cases, the air was filled with a kind of excitement unlike anything they had ever experienced in their young lives.

This spirit led more than a thousand white students to travel first to Oxford, Ohio, in June for training by battle-hardened SNCC workers at the Oxford College for Women. They needed the students to know that this project was no picnic. They talked to them about fear that they themselves lived with constantly and how to overcome it. There was a real reason to fear. In the months prior to the launch of the voting drive, blacks in Mississippi had been subjected to what civil rights officials described as "a reign of terror." Some of the worst things happened in the southeast corner of the state, where at least six blacks were murdered over a period of months. There were many beatings, and thirty-five black churches and some homes and businesses were burned or fire bombed. It was in Mississippi that Louis Allen, who had witnessed the killing of Herbert Lee, had been murdered by a state representative. The murder was called "justifiable homicide." These violent acts were carried out to try and repel what "many whites refer[ed] to as 'the coming invasion.'"

The students were told about the widespread violence, and they practiced role playing in which they were confronted with "angry mobs" and taught how to react nonviolently. Only a few pulled out. The SNCC organizers were thrilled that so many white students responded to their appeal. They were convinced that the presence of these students in Mississippi would attract widespread media attention. They also believed it would cause federal officials to be more vigilant. So one group of students was asked to travel to Washington before going to Mississippi to appeal to government officials to protect those involved in the voter registration effort. And the others—upward of 1,000— left for Mississippi.

The weather was blistering hot that summer, and so was the racial temperature. White resisters to integration were armed with anger and shotguns. The young people were armed only with idealism and a desire to be where the action was. There was plenty of both action and need. At the time, only 6.7 percent of blacks were registered to vote. Blacks who attempted to register were given a test that was designed to allow the registrars maximum subjective discretion. Even blacks with advanced degrees often failed the tests, while illiterate whites were unashamedly given a pass by the white registrar. The project had its work cut out for it.

The umbrella organization that provided logistics for Freedom Summer was the Council of Federated Organizations (COFO), which was based in Jackson, the capitol city. The organization received money for the project from the Atlanta-based Voter Education Project and then dispensed it to the participating organizations. They were SNCC, which had the most feet in the street; CORE; the SCLC; and the NAACP Legal Defense Fund. And each had specific tasks.

The voter registration drive lasted for two months, with SNCC and CORE fanning out throughout Mississippi to conduct voter registration campaigns. The students joined some 200 field workers, assigned to cover around eighty counties. The COFO program also drew in 200 clergymen, 200 teachers, and 150 lawyers from the NAACP Legal Defense Fund. Law students from the North volunteered as law clerks to help the legal team.

The group also established Freedom Schools in an effort to raise the literacy levels for black high school students, who had until then been educated (or mis-educated) in separate and unequal schools. By the end of the summer, 2,500 African Americans in Mississippi would attend the Freedom Schools.

But perhaps the most audacious effort of the Freedom Summer was the plan to put together a slate of black Democrats to challenge the seating of the all-white Democratic Party slate at the Democratic National Convention at the end of the summer.

Among the students who went south was Michael Schwerner, a Cornell University graduate who went with his wife, Rita, to work for CORE. They settled in Meridian, Mississippi, and opened a community center to help black children learn to read and write and also to encourage their parents to register to vote. James Chaney was a twenty-one-year-old plasterer in Meridian who often dropped in at the center, becoming a close friend of the twenty-four-year-old Schwerner.

On June 21, 1964, Schwerner and Chaney, along with a new arrival, Andrew Goodman, a twenty-year-old college student from New York, went to Neshoba County, according to Bob Moses, to look for housing for volunteers and to scout churches where they might hold meetings. At the time, the danger from white racists was so great that any volunteer out in the field was supposed to call in every half hour. If the call didn't come within fifteen minutes after the end of the half hour, recalled civil rights activist Sandra Cason, there was a system in place that involved calling the FBI and the Justice Department and the local police. The call from Goodman, Schwerner, and Chaney did not come. After an hour of not hearing from them, it became clear they were either in serious danger or dead.

SNCC workers back in Oxford became concerned. At some point, they heard the three had been arrested in Neshoba County. But the local police insisted that they had been released. The wife of Michael Schwerner asked the students to help put pressure on the Justice Department to look into what had happened to them.

Two days after they went missing, national attention and pressure from the young men's parents led President Lyndon B. Johnson to send Allen Dulles, a former head of the Central Intelligence Agency, to Mississippi to meet with Governor Paul Johnson and help direct the search.

During the search, many bodies of blacks who had mysteriously disappeared were found around the county. It was a gutwrenching time for the nation and especially for the civil rights community, myself included. I still identified closely with the young people in the movement. As the hours passed and there was no word of the young men, I had a sinking feeling they were dead. What else could it be? And so, like the rest of America, I waited anxiously for word. The word was a long time coming. It finally came, forty-four days later, on August 4. I picked up the newspaper and there was the story. The headline in *The*

Created less than a month after the rights workers' bodies were found, a poster commemorates their ultimate sacrifice for the movement.

New York Times heralded a tragic ending to the forty-four days of anxiety and hope: "Graves at a Dam." The lead on the story, written by journalist Claude Sitton, a veteran civil rights reporter, while still couched in speculation, came close to closing the mystery of the disappearance of the three: "Bodies believed to be those of three civil rights workers missing since June 21 were found early tonight near Philadelphia, Miss." It went on to explain that the three bodies had been found in a fresh earthen dam a few miles outside Philadelphia, Mississippi. The most chilling paragraph for me was the one that described the removal of the bodies. "The bodies were then sealed in plastic bags and brought by ambulance to the University of Mississippi Medical Center in Jackson." It was the words "sealed in plastic bags" that more than almost anything else spoke to the finality of three young lives and sent tears rolling down my cheeks. At that moment I didn't care who saw them. But my office mates were equally somber. I could only hope that Martin Luther King's preaching about "redemptive suffering" would be a consolation to the dead men's colleagues and their families, especially since it would be years before the killers would be brought to any semblance of justice.

A later investigation revealed that the killing had been planned by a local minister, and that the killers were members of the White Citizens Council and the Ku Klux Klan. Even though they hated all three of the civil rights workers enough to murder them, they clearly hated the young black man, James Chaney, the most. They shot the other two with one bullet to the heart, but they first beat Chaney, breaking both his arms and his jaw and delivering blows to his groin. They shot him three times.

The deadly violence was not only measured in the deaths of Goodman, Chaney, and Schwerner. When their bodies were found, thanks to a tip-off by an informant paid by the FBI, so were seven other bodies of black men who had disappeared at different times without a trace. And COFO went on to compile a list of other atrocities during that summer: at least four people had been shot and wounded, fifty-two beaten or otherwise injured, and some 250 arrested. By the end of the summer, there would be four murders and sixty black churches would be burned, marking a vengeful resurgence of the violent white supremacist Ku

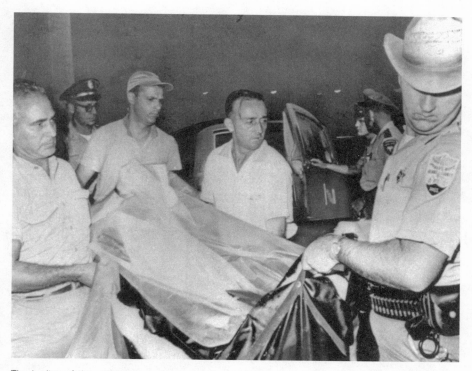

The bodies of the civil rights workers were carried from a dam in Neshoba County, Mississippi, on August 4, 1964.

Klux Klan. But while civil rights activists in the South were devastated, they continued to live by their commitment to "keep on keepin' on."

The summer ended with few changes that could be measured. Of the 900,000 blacks in the state, only a handful actually registered to vote. But Mississippi had changed—it was no longer the feared and impenetrable bastion of white supremacy. The young black Mississippians had found their footing and had emboldened many of their parents. More black people than ever before had reached a new determination to topple the white political power structure.

Moreover, the groundwork had been laid for blacks, like the whites they lived among, to have a voice in their own lives. In April 1964, the new political party had been formed to represent the black masses. It was called The Mississippi Freedom Democratic Party (MFDP).

An integrated group, the MFDP had as its goal to unseat the all-white delegation at the Democratic National Convention in August. But the leaders of the party were still afraid of losing their large voting base of white Southerners. In fact, Texas governor John Connally insisted, "Don't let those baboons walk onto the convention floor." In the end, the Credentials Committee offered to seat two of the MFDP delegates. The group refused to compromise, insisting that their entire delegation be seated. In the end, they were denied representation. They staged a protest on the floor of the convention, singing the freedom songs that had sustained the civil rights activists through thick and thin. John Lewis remembered this as a critical moment in the history of the civil rights movement.

As far as I'm concerned, this was the turning point of the civil rights movement. I'm absolutely convinced of that. Until then, despite every setback and disappointment and obstacle we had faced over the years, the belief still prevailed that the system would work, the system would listen, the system would respond. Now, for the first time, we had made our way to the very center of the system. We had played by the rules, done everything we were supposed to do, had played the game exactly as required, had arrived at the doorstep and found the door slammed in our face.

But the people of the movement were not yet ready to give up on the system. A civil rights bill had been making its way through Congress, and civil rights heroes like Fannie Lou Hamer and SCLC's Arnelle Ponder cornered members of Congress, helping them understand what the bill meant. Hamer shared her story, telling Congress:

I traveled twenty-six miles to the county courthouse to try to register to become a first-class citizen. I was fired the thirty-first of August in

Members of the Mississippi Freedom Democratic Party arrived in Atlantic City for the Democratic Convention, hoping to unseat the all-white Mississippi delegation on August 21.

1962 from a plantation where I had worked as a timekeeper and a share-cropper for eighteen years. My husband had worked thirty years.

I was met by my children when I returned from the courthouse, and my girl and my husband's cousin told me that this man my husband worked for was raising a lot of Cain. I went on in the house and it wasn't too long before my husband came and said this plantation owner said I would have to leave if I didn't go down and withdraw. About that time, the man walked up, Mr. Marlowe, and he said, "Is Fannie Lou back yet?" My husband said, "She is." I walked out of the house at this time. He said, "Fannie Lou, you have been to the courthouse to try to register," and he said, "We are not ready for this in Mississippi." I said, "I didn't register for you, I tried to register for myself."

After signing the Civil Rights Bill on July 2, 1964, President Johnson handed one of the pens he used to Dr. King.

While Mrs. Hamer suffered more than most in the denial of her rights, hers stood as the story of all the disenfranchised black voters throughout the South.

Many Southerners opposed the bill, including Senator Richard B. Russell, who had spoken at my graduation in 1963. He filibustered for fifty-four days, and warned President Johnson that passage of the bill "will not only cost you the South, it will cost you the election." (It didn't, thanks to newly enfranchised black voters.) And Senator Barry Goldwater spoke the words I had heard from Southern white students opposed to my court-ordered entry into the University of Georgia: "You can't legislate morality." This was the defiant cry of those who insisted that no amount of federal intervention would make them change their belief in segregation and the inferiority of blacks.

Still, on July 2, 1964, President Johnson, a Southerner from Texas, signed into law the civil rights bill that the late President Kennedy had set in motion, giving, as Andrew Young recalled, "the strongest civil rights speech ever given by an American President."

The bill outlawed discrimination in schools, public places, and in hiring. And it also outlawed discrimination on the basis of gender, giving women as much of a victory as African Americans.

Johnson had gotten the wish he made when he delivered his first State of the Union Address, when he had urged Congress to "let this session be known as the session which did more for Civil Rights than a hundred sessions combined." It was the most far-reaching civil rights act since Reconstruction. Ironically, in death, James Chaney, Andrew Goodman, and Michael Schwerner could take a large part of the credit. But neither President Johnson, nor the people of the movement, were finished yet.

And I was just beginning. On August 1, *The New Yorker* published my first writing effort since I joined the magazine. It was the lead piece in the magazine, the Notes and Comment section, and it told of the aftermath of a riot in a black section of Brooklyn known as Bedford Stuyvesant. Although it was descriptive, it also drew upon my Southern civil-rights-bred consciousness as it looked beyond the South at more pervasive racial discrimination that would eventually lead to racial flare-ups across the East and Midwest. It would be the first of many pieces in my career that would focus on discrimination against black people and their efforts to change things—and not just in the South. But for now, I was ecstatic over being published, if not over the reasons why.

Then, in December, the movement received a major international blessing. Thirty-seven-year-old Martin Luther King, Jr., became the youngest man ever to be awarded the Nobel Peace Prize. It was given for his work to end segregation though nonviolence.

News to Print"

The New Yo

..No. 39,127.

© 1965 by The New York Times Company.
Times Square, New York, N. Y. 10036

NEW YORK, WEDNESDAY,

OWN
OSAL
ARLEY

t No Bid
scussion
' Ends

N OPEN

Peaceful
Troops
ctory

KEL

s Times
larch 9—
as told U
y General
ns, that it
any other
erence on
Vietnam
to halt its

Ir. Thant's
ven-nation
sion was
the State
accompa-
thanks for
essions of
channels
r a peace-

, Govern-
a major
repulse
ult on a
270 miles

Kerr Is Resigning At U. of California; Aide Also Leaving

Clark Kerr

By WALLACE TURNER
Special to The New York Times

BERKELEY, Calif., March 9—Clark Kerr announced today his intention to resign as president of the University of California. Martin Meyerson announced that he would resign as acting chancellor of the Berkeley campus.

Neither man would answer questions beyond the brief statements handed out at a hurriedly convened news conference in University Hall, where Mr. Kerr has his offices.

Mr. Kerr, 53 years old, is responsible for the entire

F.P.C., 3-1, GRANTS CON ED A LICENSE FOR HUDSON PLANT

Damage to Scenic Values Is Discounted—Rep. Ottinger Sees a Court Challenge

By WARREN WEAVER Jr.
Special to The New York Times

WASHINGTON, March 9—The Federal Power Commission today granted the Consolidated Edison Company a license to build the world's largest pumped-storage hydroelectric power plant on the banks of the Hudson River near Cornwall.

Conservation groups had strongly opposed giving the utility permission for the $162 million project, maintaining that it would spoil the beauty of the Hudson highlands.

One of the power plant's chief opponents, Representative Richard L. Ottinger of Westchester County, said today he was sure that there would be a court challenge of the commission decision.

Ross the Dissenter

The commission divided 3 to 1 on the issue, with Commissioner Charles R. Ross dissenting. He called for further hearings on aspects of the controversy and no decision before March 1, 1966.

[Residents of Cornwall-on-Hudson were pleased by the decision and Consolidated

DR. KING STATE P UNDER

LATE CITY EDITION

U. S. Weather Bureau Report (Page 82) forecasts:
Fair and cooler today; clear,
cold tonight and tomorrow.
Temp. range: 40—37; yesterday: 53—40.

CH 10, 1965.

TEN CENTS

EADS MARCH AT SELMA;
LICE END IT PEACEABLY
U.S.-ARRANGED ACCORD

1,500 TURNED BACK

Protest Begun Despite Court—3 Ministers Attacked Later

Text of Federal court order will be found on Page 22.

By ROY REED
Special to The New York Times

SELMA, Ala., March 9—The Rev. Dr. Martin Luther King Jr. led 1,500 Negroes and whites on a second attempted protest march today. State troopers turned them back on the outskirts of Selma, after they had gone one mile.

But this time there was no violence—unlike a similar confrontation at the same spot on Sunday. Then, troopers and Dallas County sheriff's officers broke up an attempted march to Montgomery, the state capital, 50 miles away, with clubs and tear gas.

1965

How long? Not long.
—*Martin Luther King, Jr., Selma, March 25, 1965*

In early February 1965, I got still another step closer to fulfilling my dream of becoming a writer. I was sitting in the office I shared with three other staff members when the phone on my desk rang.

"Miss Hunter," I heard the soft-spoken voice on the other line begin. "This is Bill Shawn. And I am calling to tell you that we liked '115th—Between Lenox and Fifth' and we would like to publish it in the magazine."

I was close to speechless. The piece he was referring to was a personal reflection in which I reached back to my childhood and the trip my grandmother and I had made from Covington, the little town in Georgia where we had once lived, to New York City. I will never forget that call or the feeling I had when I saw my name appear in the same *New Yorker* issue as Calvin Trillin, who had covered my entry into the University of Georgia for *Time* magazine four years earlier. He had since joined the staff of *The New Yorker*, and his first piece for the magazine

Facing page: State troopers stood on the steps of the Alabama state capitol, in Montgomery, denying the Selma marchers access to the governor, March 25, 1965.

Previous pages: The New York Times front page from March 10, 1965. For full text of Selma article, see page 169.

had been an extended piece of reporting on the desegregation of UGA and its aftermath, in what was titled "An Education in Georgia." Equally exciting was that my name would also appear in the same magazine as my literary hero, J. D. Salinger. I was over the moon. Yet, developments in the civil rights struggle helped keep me grounded.

In 1965, Selma, Alabama, seemed an unlikely place to stage one of the biggest demonstrations in the history of the civil rights movement. It was a kind of one-horse town, with a bridge and a main street. But soon that bridge was to become a rallying point for thousands of civil rights demonstrators from all over the country. It was in Selma that Barack Obama, in his campaign for the presidency, paid tribute to the giants on whose shoulders he said he stood.

Selma lay in the heart of the Black Belt, so named initially because of its rich black topsoil. The area was the home of the founder of the Ku Klux Klan. Blacks there could not enter the economic mainstream and were confined to working as laborers in the cotton fields, in the white folks' kitchens, and in their gardens. Black people hadn't had a voice in the affairs of the town since a black man from there served in Congress during Reconstruction. Blacks had not challenged all this, although they didn't always suffer their condition gladly. C. L. Chestnut, a black attorney from Selma, put it this way: "The first struggle would be against black fear, not white resistance."

And there were good reasons for that fear. White authorities used force and brutality against even small infractions by blacks.

As Martin Luther King aide Andrew Young put it, "[Residents of Selma] were like the dog who gets kicked all the time and who just moves out of the way whenever someone comes along." But, Young went on, "by 1965, the dog had been kicked too many times . . . Selma had been bruised and abused long enough."

That's when people like Amelia Boynton, one of the few blacks registered to vote, decided to call for help. At that time, only about 2 percent of blacks of voting age were registered in Alabama. SNCC had held a Freedom Day in Selma in 1963 following the church bombing in Birmingham. On the night of the bombing, SNCC's Diane Nash had vowed to get back at Alabama governor

George Wallace and the police chief, but in a nonviolent way: SNCC would register enough black voters to drive them from office. And she set about working to keep her word.

SNCC had taken its first voter registration campaign to Selma in 1963, when registration took place only two days out of the month. There, Bernard Lafayette and his wife, Colia, had set up shop for the organization. There was a Negro Voters' League at the time, but there was little to show for their work. So Lafayette told them, "You people have been working to get more people registered, I'm here to help you."

A young man displays the marchers' message.

The twenty-two-year-old had also led by example. One night, he was stopped by two white men who told him their car wouldn't start. As he was about to help them, they hit him in the head over and over with the butt of a rifle, almost killing him.

C. L. Chestnut recalled seeing Lafayette the next day: "His eyes were all swollen, face bruised, blood all over his shirt. 'You need to go clean yourself up,' I said. 'No way,' he told me. 'This is the symbol we need.' He wore the T-shirt with caked up blood for two or three weeks, and this was a sort of turning point in terms of public sympathy in black Selma. Even the blacks who were most apprehensive about him couldn't help but respect his commitment and courage."

The example of the Lafayettes inspired thirty-two black school teachers to try and register to vote, knowing that there would be consequences. And there were. They were fired by the all-white school board. In October 1963, Lafayette and SNCC chairman John Lewis accompanied to the courthouse around 300 black people, including many elderly. But at the end of the day, only five people had been allowed to take the literacy test. Lewis, who had carried a sign calling for "One man, one vote," Lafayette, and a few others were badly beaten by the police and arrested. At that point, the court issued an injunction making it unlawful for more than three people to talk or walk down the street together.

Amelia Boynton knew well how the white registrars systematically excluded blacks from registering with bogus tests and through their own subjective decisions. But Boynton, who got along well with the SNCC activists, realized that she and they needed more help. So she called on King's SCLC. The SCLC usually avoided areas where SNCC was positioned, but together with SNCC and Boynton's banned NAACP, a full-on voter registration campaign began.

On February 1, 1965, Dr. King told an assembled crowd at the Brown Chapel AME Church, "We must be willing to go to jail by the thousands. We are not on our knees begging for the ballot. We are demanding the ballot."

On that day, up to 700 marched and were arrested, including Dr. King and Rev. Abernathy, and many high school students. But they weren't put in jail. Instead, the sheriff frog-marched the young people into the countryside, making them move so fast some even vomited.

The movement continued in Selma and spread out to other Black Belt towns, with marches and demonstrations by people who were beginning to see the real possibility of freedom. The whites of Alabama, however, were not yet ready to concede defeat. Instead, they continued their attacks on the demonstrators. On the night of February 18, an Alabama state trooper shot a protestor named Jimmie Lee Jackson. Twenty-six-year-old Jackson was a deacon in his church and a Vietnam War veteran. He and his family were participating in a nighttime demonstration. When police began attacking the demonstrators, Jackson, his mother, and his grandfather, who were under attack, retreated to a nearby black café. After the police beat his eighty-two-year-old grandfather to the floor, Jackson tried to protect his mother. He was grabbed by a state trooper and shot twice in the stomach. He died two days later. And, as Andrew Young would later recall, his death "set the stage for the climax of our Selma campaign."

Within days, Dr. King and others organized a march that was intended to go fifty-four miles from Selma to the capital in Montgomery, where demonstrators hoped to put their grievances before the governor. They also wanted to ask about the governor's role in the violence that took Jimmie Lee Jackson's life.

SNCC was not in favor of the march, fearing the potential toll from police violence. But SNCC's John Lewis, once again, put his well-battered body on the line. On that day, Sunday, March 7, Lewis was in the lead, along with the SCLC's Hosea Williams, as a throng of some 400 mostly black people, including at least one eight-year-old girl, Sheyann Webb, headed out from the Brown Chapel AME Church toward Selma's one bridge.

When the marchers crossed the Edmund Pettus Bridge, waiting for them on the other side was an untold number of Alabama state troopers, some on horseback. The troopers gave a warning that the march was unlawful, and in a flash waded into the demonstrators, beating them with billy clubs and bullwhips. They also

Marchers crossing the Edmund Pettus Bridge were met by Alabama state troopers, who attacked them with clubs, bullwhips, and tear gas.

set off tear gas and trampled some demonstrators with the horses. According to one protestor, C. L. Chestnut, "It looked like a battlefield."

John Lewis and Amelia Boynton were knocked unconscious, and Lewis sustained a fractured skull. But they, along with all the other injured and frightened demonstrators, managed to get back to the church where they had started the march.

After that harrowing day, Sunday, March 7, became known as "Bloody Sunday." But for those in the movement, like Lewis and SNCC in particular, the sacrifice was worth it. They had counted on the terrifying images of the victims being flashed around the nation and the world, believing they would draw even more support from people of all races and colors. And the world reacted. The violence that day opened a new chapter in the civil rights saga, sounding what would become the death knell for Jim Crow.

Although their spirits were low, the demonstrators were determined to finish the march. Dr. King, who had not participated, flew in from Atlanta and re-energized the crowd with these words:

Somebody's asking, . . .

How long will justice be crucified, "and truth bear it?" I come to say to you this afternoon, however difficult the moment, however frustrating the hour, it will not be long, because "truth crushed to earth will rise again." How long? Not long, because "no lie can live forever." How long? Not long. How long? Because "you shall reap what you sow."

And then Dr. King asked the question that he had borrowed from an abolitionist preacher, and which President Obama would borrow some fifty years later in reaction to the violence the Iranian state unleashed on its people after its disputed 2009 election: "How long? Not long, because the arc of the moral universe is long, but it bends toward justice."

It was a powerful speech that not only sent local marchers back into the streets, but inspired people from all over the country. Black and white, young and old, celebrities and ordinary people were moved by the sight of such rank injustice to join the cause.

Leaving Selma, the Great Freedom March was greeted by jeering bystanders and hostile signs, and kept right on going.

Over the next few days, two more marches took place. The first met the same phalanx of state troopers as before, but rather than attempting to go forward, the demonstrators knelt down in front of the troopers and prayed. At this point, Dr. King's group did not want to violate a federal court order against continuing the march. They had always believed they would get more justice out of the federal courts than the local ones and wanted to keep the federal judges, if not on their side, at least not against them. The SNCC group and some in the SCLC didn't agree, but were overruled. So the marchers survived to march another day. Only James Reeb didn't. Reeb, a white Unitarian Universalist minister from Boston, was caught by a group of whites as he was walking in the streets that night, having taken a wrong turn. He was beaten badly by the police with their clubs. The local Selma hospital refused him treatment, so he had to be taken to a hospital two hours away in Birmingham. He died two days later.

Despite that tragedy, Dr. King's restraint was rewarded. Federal judge Frank Johnson ruled that the marchers had the right to demonstrate and prohibited the state from interfering. It took five days for them to walk from Selma to Montgomery, but they did it under the protection of the Alabama National Guard, which President Johnson had federalized.

As he stood on the steps of the state capitol, with some 25,000 marchers in front of him, Dr. King spoke of his faith that the war was almost over, and his vision for its end: "Our aim must never be to defeat or humiliate the white man, but to win his friendship and understanding. We must come to see that the end we seek is a society at peace with itself, a society that can live with its conscience." And, characteristic cadence rising, he continued: I know you are asking today, *How long will it take?* I come to say to you this afternoon, however difficult the moment, however frustrating the hour, it will not be long."

Later that night came a difficult moment, a frustrating hour. After driving some of the marchers home, one of the group, Viola Liuzzo, was shot in the face and killed. In the assailants' car were Ku Klux Klansmen and an undercover FBI agent. Earlier, the white mother of five had left her family and driven alone from Detroit to join the march, one of the many whites who expressed their support with their feet. Some, like Liuzzo, paid with their lives.

For all intents and purposes, the Selma to Montgomery march was the end of the Selma voting rights drive. But it was in a real sense the crowning achievement of the civil rights movement. Within a few months, the reverberations from "Bloody Sunday" would lead to the Voting Rights Act of 1965, which opened the door to the long corridor that led Barack Obama to the White House in January 2009. His election could not have happened without the pressure and the sacrifices of the leaders and the foot soldiers of the civil rights movement—the leaders' names were well known to the world, but the names of many in the trenches will never be known.

The Voting Rights Act was also a credit to a Southern president, Lyndon

Baines Johnson. Once elected to the presidency, he had used the most powerful bully pulpit of them all to ensure its passage. It was a week after "Bloody Sunday," March 15, 1965.

President Johnson stood before a joint session of Congress and eloquently decried the violence of Selma, saying there was "no pride" in what had happened there. He eloquently saluted those fighting for their rights, defining not only his vision of America, but her core and her challenge. "For the cries of pain and the hymns and protests of oppressed people have summoned into convocation all the majesty of this great government—the government of the greatest nation on earth." He decried the killing of James Reeb, whom he called "one good man . . . a man of God," and spoke of many issues that challenged the mission of America— war and peace, prosperity and depression. But, he said, "Rarely in any time does an issue lay bare the secret heart of America itself . . . the issue of equal rights for American Negroes is such an issue."

Then, President Johnson delivered lines that would resonate throughout the world and send a message especially to the Deep South resisters:

> And should we defeat every enemy, and should we double our wealth and conquer the stars, and still be unequal to this issue, then we will have failed as a people and as a nation. For, with a country as with a person, "what is a man profited if he shall gain the whole world, and lose his own soul?" There is no Negro problem. There is no Southern problem. There is no Northern problem. There is only an American problem.

Johnson didn't stop with that bit of soaring oratory. He went on to end his speech with words no one would have expected to hear from his lips, words that up to that point had been only the watchwords of the civil rights movement:

> But even if we pass this bill the battle will not be over. What happened in Selma is part of a far larger movement, which reaches into every section and state of America. It is the effort of American Negroes to secure for

Before signing the Civil Rights Bill, President Lyndon Johnson addressed members of Congress on August 6, 1965.

themselves the full blessings of American life. Their cause must be our cause too. Because it's not just Negroes, but really it's all of us, who must overcome the crippling legacy of bigotry and injustice. And we shall overcome.

Dr. King, who was in the audience, was as shocked as anyone to hear those words coming from the president of the United States. His own emotion was betrayed by a tear that rolled down his cheek.

King was moved not just by Johnson's appropriation of the movement's mantra, but also the content of the bill. It promised to wipe out literacy tests and other barriers aimed specifically at barring blacks from registering to vote. At the time, more than 2 million blacks of voting age were unregistered.

Later, the president invited the black leaders who had come to hear the speech into the rotunda. Among them were Dr. King, CORE's James Farmer, and the NAACP's Roy Wilkins. John Lewis from SNCC was also included, representing all those young people like himself whose foresight, courage, bravery, hard heads, and commitment to nonviolence had sparked a revolution that had taken them all to this, the highest mountaintop.

By this time, I had been promoted to *The New Yorker* writing staff as its first black reporter for "Talk of the Town," the magazine's first section. And I set about trying to continue the goals of the movement in my own way. The second story I wrote was a fictionalized account of a real incident involving a white city official, my grandmother, and her efforts to maintain the grave of my grandfather in a segregated cemetery in Covington, Georgia, where we had lived until I was about ten. I had begun to learn how to do as a professional writer what I had done as a civil rights pioneer. And deep in my soul, I knew that commitment would be with me from mountaintop to mountaintop.

After *The New Yorker* I went on to work for the NBC television affiliate in Washington, DC, and later *The New York Times*, where this photo was taken.

In the years to come, as a reporter for *The New York Times,* the *McNeil/Lehrer News Hour,* National Public Radio, and CNN, I would travel the world looking for and finding people who needed a voice to help them gain their rights, their freedom, and their human dignity. I found them in the Harlems of America and in the West Bank and Gaza and in Israel, in Grenada and Somalia, in Haiti, and all over the continent of Africa. I first visited South Africa in 1985 as hundreds of thousands of the country's mostly black people were engaged in a decades-long struggle for their full rights, suffering some of the same brutality and viciousness at the hands of the white minority regime as their brothers and sisters in America's Deep South. And what a joy it was to sit with Nelson Mandela in 1990, shortly after he was released from serving twenty-seven years in prison for fighting for his people's rights, and to share with him our common history of struggle and its victorious end. By this time, however, I had learned the truth of a Haitian proverb that goes: *Deye mon geye mon.* Beyond the mountain more mountains. While we could still rejoice in our victories, we had to "keep on keepin' on," sharing our history so that future generations can be empowered by the giants on whose shoulders they stand, and sing, if it becomes necessary, "Ain't gonna let nobody turn me 'roun'."

"All the News.
t's Fit to Print"

The New Y

CXIV ... No. 39,277.
© 1965 by The New York Times Company,
Times Square, New York, N. Y. 10036
NEW YORK, SATU

NG APPEAL TH VIETNAM EN AND AID

ont of Guerrillas pen Assistance nsify the War

RMS RESTATED

Bar Negotiation hey Participate ecisive Voice'

ietcong statement ound on Page 2.

e Associated Press
Saturday, Aug. 7 —
1 front of the Viet-
llas in South Viet-
ked North Vietnam
assistance against
tes forces in the
for preparations to
to battle, the Hanoi
ed today.
which has said it
volunteers if asked,
etcong statement as
that the guerrillas

Associated Press Wirephoto

CONFER ON ASIA: Alex Quaison-Sackey, Foreign Minister of Ghana, hands a letter from President Kwame Nkrumah to President Johnson in White House. Mr. Quaison-Sackey said message should promote peace in Vietnam.

Nkrumah Note on Vietnam Is Delivered to President

By RICHARD EDER

ENGINEER WARN CITY CAN RUN OU OF WATER IN 19

Commission Told of Dan in Measures to Protec Philadelphia Supply

By McCANDLISH PHILLI
Special to The New York Times

PHILADELPHIA, Aug. 6
New York City told the D
ware River Basin Commis
today that the city could '
out of water by the middle
February, 1966," if adverse
ditions continued.

Demands now being pla
upon the city's diminish
water supplies constitute w
is "actually not safe operati
Edward J. Clark, the c
chief water engineer, decla
at a special emergency m
ing of the commission here
day.

But Mr. Clark acknowle
that for the city to come w
in the margin of safe op
tion, it would have to take
tions that would endanger
water supplies of Philadel
and Camden.

Holding Back Salt Wat

Sea water driven by tide
threatening to invade a P
delphia water intake on

ork Times.

, AUGUST 7, 1965.

LATE CITY EDI

U. S. Weather Bureau Report (Page 4
Sunny, hot, humid today, fai
Partly cloudy and hot ton

Temp. Range: 92—70; yesterda
Temp.-Hum. Index: near 80; yest

TEN C

OHNSON SIGNS VOTING RIGHTS BIL
ORDERS IMMEDIATE ENFORCEMEN
4 SUITS WILL CHALLENGE POLL T

THE ROTUNDA: President Johnson speaks at Capitol before signing Voting Rights Act. To left are dev

United Press Internati

EPILOGUE

The Voting Rights Act of 1965 opened doors long shut in the South, where half of the blacks in the United States lived. And Southern blacks eagerly walked through those doors, taking their places in the corridors of political power—at the local, state, and national levels. Within five years of the passage of the act, close to 1,500 blacks had been elected to public office. By 1970, there were 48 black mayors, 575 other city officials, 362 school board members, 168 state legislators, 114 judges and magistrates, and 99 other black law enforcement officials. Moreover, Edward W. Brook of Massachusetts became the first black elected to the U.S. Senate since Reconstruction, and nine blacks were elected to the House of Representatives.

My native Georgia had two black senators and twelve representatives by 1970, the largest number of black legislators in the South, and would in 1973 elect

Facing page: After being sworn in as the first black associate justice on September 1, 1967, Thurgood Marshall posed on the Supreme Court steps, this time with his wife, Cecilia, and sons, Thurgood Marshall, Jr., and John.

Previous pages: *The New York Times* front page from August 7, 1965. For full text of Voting Rights Act article, see page 173.

thirty-five-year-old Maynard Jackson as the first black mayor of a Southern city, Atlanta (the same year Coleman Young became the first black mayor of a Northern city: Detroit, Michigan). Civil rights activist Jesse Jackson called Maynard Jackson's election "the fruits of a political renaissance."

That renaissance also led to the election of a man whose nonviolent fight for rights in Albany, Georgia, caused him to be slapped unconscious by a deputy sheriff and put in a cold jail cell in 1961. That civil rights activist, Charles Sherrod, was elected in 1976 to Albany's city commission.

In Birmingham, Alabama, two blacks stepped into political prominence: Arthur Shores was appointed to the city council in 1968, and Richard Arrington became mayor in 1979.

SNCC's Marion Barry, who left his native Deep South after working to organize black voters, went to Washington, D.C. There he continued to use his movement organizing skills to help the poor. He was elected as the second black mayor of Washington, D.C., in 1979 and went on to serve four terms. In 1980, my high school classmate and longtime friend, Carolyn Long (now Banks), took a seat on the Atlanta city council as its first African American member.

And John Lewis, who never retreated from a blow on his long quest for justice, was elected in 1981 to the Atlanta city council and, in 1986, ran a successful campaign for Congress against former SNCC colleague Julian Bond. Bond went on to serve for twenty years in the Georgia legislature. I interviewed him for *The New Yorker* after he had served the first year of his two-year term. He was at the time introducing legislation for the official recognition of Black History Week. And Lewis, who also remained true to his beliefs in justice and equality and the moral principles that guided his movement work, came to be known as the "conscience of the Congress." He opened still more doors as a member of the House Ways and Means Committee, Congress's chief tax writing committee. He also serves on its subcommittee on Income Security and Family Support.

After Barack Obama had taken the oath of office for president of the United States, *New Yorker* editor David Remnick reported that Lewis approached President

On September 3, 1986, having beaten his old SNCC colleague Julian Bond in a run-off election, John Lewis (left) and his wife, Lillian, celebrated his election to Congress.

Obama with a commemorative photograph and asked him to sign it. The president wrote, "Because of you, John. Barack Obama."

It is not possible to name the tens of thousands of Americans—black and white—Obama could have written these words to. Nor do we even know many of them who worked quietly but effectively and courageously for their rights. The lesson in those words for future generations is the importance of knowing where they—and their country—came from, so they can see more clearly where they are going, and can be armed with historical confidence in how to success-fully face challenges. The battle for civil and human rights is ongoing all over the world, and here at home, where we have yet to reach a post-racial society. That battle still needs new, committed foot soldiers to enlist. There will, no doubt, still be "some difficult days ahead," but history can point the way.

History now records, for example, long-delayed justice for some, though not all, of the movement's martyrs. The Justice Department is pursuing at least 108 unsolved or inadequately solved civil rights–era murders through its Civil Rights Era Cold Case Initiative, begun in 2007. And although all-white juries in the past failed to convict some of the apprehended civil rights–era murderers, years later, thanks to the work of groups like the Southern Poverty Law Center and the Civil Rights and Restorative Justice Project, some of them were finally made to pay for their crimes.

Among them are the following:

Byron De La Beckwith was sentenced to life in prison in 1994 for the mur-der of Medgar Evers.

In 1997, **Michael Lee Farley** and **Larry Joe Sims**—two men who had received suspended sentences after gunning down thirteen-year-old Virgil Ware following the September 15, 1963, Birmingham church bombing—apologized to the Ware family.

Klansman **Thomas Blanton, Jr.**, was sentenced to life in prison in 2001, and **Bobby Frank Cherry** received the same sentence in 2002 for the 1963 bombing of Sixteenth Street Baptist Church, resulting in the death of four little girls.

In 2005, **Edgar Ray Killen**, a former member of the Ku Klux Klan, was found guilty of manslaughter in the killing of Goodman, Chaney, and Schwer-ner, with a mixed-race jury saying there was not enough evidence to convict him of murder. He was sentenced to sixty years in prison.

In 2007, **James Ford Seal** was convicted of murdering two black teenagers—Charles Eddie Moore and Henry Hezekiah—in 1964. They were

On January 7, 2005, Edgar Ray Killen was found guilty of manslaughter in the 1964 killing of the civil rights workers Schwerner, Chaney, and Goodman.

severely beaten and thrown into the Mississippi River while they were still alive. Seal was sentenced to three life terms. An appeal was later denied in 2009.

Also in 2007, federal officials announced they were reopening more cases. Some twenty cases have been reopened and many of them retried. And others are still being pursued by a generation that has accepted the call of history to carry on the mission of the civil rights movement.

TIMELINE

1787—A compromise results in blacks being defined as "three-fifths of a person" in the U.S. Constitution.

1857—The three-fifths compromise is upheld in the case of *Dred Scott v. Sandford*. The Supreme Court declares "any person descended from Africans is not a citizen."

1870—The Fifteenth Amendment is ratified, granting voting rights to all male citizens regardless of "race, color, or previous condition of servitude."

1896—The Dred Scott decision is upheld by the U.S. Supreme Court in the case of *Plessy v. Ferguson*.

July 18, 1947—India is granted independence from British rule, largely as a result of nonviolent protest tactics taught by Mahatma Gandhi.

September 25, 1951—Herbert Lee is shot and killed by E. H. Hurst, a white member of the Mississippi legislature, who claims self-defense.

November 7, 1955—The Supreme Court rules in favor of Sarah Keys in *Keys v. Carolina Coach Company*, confirming that it is illegal to segregate buses traveling across state lines

December 1, 1955—Rosa Parks refuses to give up her bus seat to a white passenger, sparking the Montgomery bus boycott.

1865—The Thirteenth Amendment is ratified, abolishing slavery.

1868—The Fourteenth Amendment guarantees equal protection of the law for all U.S. citizens.

1909—The National Association for the Advancement of Colored People (NAACP) is founded.

1938—The U.S. Supreme Court orders the law school at the University of Missouri to admit Lloyd Gaines or provide separate but equal facilities, in the case of *Gaines v. Canada*.

May 17, 1954—A decision is handed down in the case of *Brown v. Board of Education of Topeka*, ruling that "separate but equal" violates the Fourteenth Amendment.

August 28, 1955—Fourteen-year-old Emmett Till is murdered in Money, Mississippi.

February 3, 1956—Autherine Lucy is admitted to the University of Alabama.

January 1957—The Southern Christian Leadership Conference (SCLC) is established, with the Rev. Martin Luther King, Jr., as its first president.

September 25, 1957—After a standoff of nearly a month, federal troops intervene on behalf of the "Little Rock Nine," forcing the integration of Central High School in Little Rock, Arkansas.

November 1959—Charlayne Hunter and Hamilton Holmes submit applications for admission to the University of Georgia.

March 9, 1960—"An Appeal for Human Rights" is published in Atlanta, Georgia, newspapers.

March 15, 1960—Students protest in the streets in Atlanta, Georgia, and arrests are made, but protests are later suspended until the fall of 1960.

October 22, 1960—Atlanta students are released from jail and a thirty-day truce is called by Mayor William B. Hartsfield.

November 1960—Four thousand student protestors hit the streets in Atlanta, Georgia, forcing closure of downtown lunch counters.

January 9, 1961—Charlayne Hunter and Hamilton Holmes enroll at the University of Georgia.

January 1961—James Meredith applies for admission to the University of Mississippi.

February 1, 1960—Joe McNeil, Junior Blair, Frank McCain, and David Richmond sit down at a Woolworth's lunch counter, launching a sit-in movement that rapidly spreads across the South.

February 13, 1960—The sit-in movement reaches Nashville, Tennessee.

April 1960—The Student Nonviolent Coordinating Committee (SNCC) is founded.

October 19 1960—Dr. Martin Luther King, Jr., joins renewed student protests in a sit-in at an Atlanta, Georgia, department store. Thirty-five people, including King, are arrested.

December 5, 1960—The U.S. Supreme Court, in *Boynton v. Virginia*, extends its 1955 desegregation order to include bus stations and toilets used by interstate passengers.

January 6, 1961—Federal judge William Bootle rules that Charlayne Hunter and Hamilton Holmes must be admitted to the University of Georgia.

March 1961—White businessmen in Atlanta agree to integrate lunch counters following court-ordered desegregation in the fall, but later renege on their promise.

May 4, 1961—Thirteen activists begin Freedom Rides from Washington, D.C., to New Orleans, planning to arrive by May 17, 1961.

July 1961—Bob Moses, field secretary for SNCC, arrives in McComb, Mississippi, and establishes a voter education program.

Summer 1961—Student demonstrations in Atlanta, Georgia, result in white businessmen closing seventy downtown stores for three months.

April 16, 1963—Martin Luther King, Jr., writes "Letter from a Birmingham Jail."

May 2–4, 1963—Children march in Birmingham, Alabama. Police Chief Bull Connor's violent suppression of the march draws international attention to the cause.

September 15, 1963—A bomb explodes at the Sixteenth Street Baptist Church in Birmingham, Alabama, killing four young girls.

October 8, 1963—Bernard Lafayette and John Lewis accompany 300 potential black voting registrants to the Selma, Alabama, courthouse. At the end of the day, only five people had been allowed to take the literacy test.

January 23, 1964—The Twenty-fourth Amendment is ratified, abolishing the poll tax.

June–August 1964—The Council of Federated Organizations (COFO) coordinates "Freedom Summer," a massive voter registration effort.

October 1, 1962—James Meredith becomes the first black student to enroll at the University of Mississippi.

April 3, 1963—The SCLC launches a boycott of downtown businesses in Birmingham, Alabama, and issues the Birmingham Manifesto.

June 12, 1963—Medgar Evers, the NAACP's Mississippi field secretary, is shot and killed.

August 28, 1963—Two hundred thousand people gather on the National Mall for the March on Washington. Martin Luther King, Jr., delivers his famous "I have a dream" speech.

October 14, 1963—Martin Luther King, Jr., thirty-five, becomes the youngest winner of the Nobel Peace Prize,

November 22, 1963—President John F. Kennedy is assassinated.

June 21, 1964—CORE members James Chaney, Andrew Goodman, and Michael Schwerner disappear while scouting housing in Neshoba County, Mississippi.

July 2, 1964—President Lyndon B. Johnson signs the Civil Rights Act, prohibiting discrimination in schools, voter registration requirements, and in places of public accommodation. As a result, Atlanta begins city-wide desegregation for the first time.

August 4, 1964—The bodies of James Chaney, Andrew Goodman, and Michael Schwerner are found.

December 10, 1964—Martin Luther King, Jr., accepts the Nobel Peace Prize in Oslo, Norway.

March 7, 1965—The Selma to Montgomery march begins and is brutally suppressed.

August 10, 1965—Congress passes the Voting Rights Act, outlawing discriminatory practices such as literacy tests in registering citizens to vote.

April 4, 1968—Martin Luther King, Jr., is shot in Memphis, Tennessee.

April 11, 1968—President Johnson signs Civil Rights Act of 1968, outlawing discrimination in housing.

January 2, 1965—Dr. King launches the Selma Voting Right Movement, telling an assembled crowd at the Brown Chapel AME Church, "We must be willing to go to jail by the thousands. We are not on our knees begging for the ballot. We are demanding the ballot."

February 18, 1965—An Alabama state trooper shoots Jimmie Lee Jackson.

September 24, 1965—President Johnson issues Executive Order 11246 enforcing affirmative action.

June 12, 1967—A Supreme Court decision in the case of *Loving v. Virginia* declares laws prohibiting interracial marriage unconstitutional.

March 4, 2007—Obama addresses a crowd at Selma, Alabama, during his campaign saying, "I'm here because some-body marched for our freedom . . . I'm here because all of you sacrificed for me. I stand on the shoulders of giants."

January 20, 2009—Barack Obama is inaugurated as the first African American president of the United States.

ARTICLES

OBAMA ELECTED PRESIDENT AS RACIAL BARRIER FALLS
By Adam Nagourney

November 4, 2008—Barack Hussein Obama was elected the 44th president of the United States on Tuesday, sweeping away the last racial barrier in American politics with ease as the country chose him as its first black chief executive.

The election of Mr. Obama amounted to a national catharsis—a repudiation of a historically unpopular Republican president and his economic and foreign policies, and an embrace of Mr. Obama's call for a change in the direction and the tone of the country.

But it was just as much a strikingly symbolic moment in the evolution of the nation's fraught racial history, a breakthrough that would have seemed unthinkable just two years ago.

Mr. Obama, 47, a first-term senator from Illinois, defeated Senator John McCain of Arizona, 72, a former prisoner of war who was making his second bid for the presidency.

To the very end, Mr. McCain's campaign was eclipsed by an opponent who was nothing short of a phenomenon, drawing huge crowds epitomized by the tens of thousands of people who turned out to hear Mr. Obama's victory speech in Grant Park in Chicago.

Mr. McCain also fought the headwinds of a relentlessly hostile political environment, weighted down with the baggage left to him by President Bush and an economic collapse that took place in the middle of the general election campaign.

"If there is anyone out there who still doubts that America is a place where all things are possible, who still wonders if the dream of our founders is alive in our time, who still questions the power of our democracy, tonight is your answer," said Mr. Obama, standing before a huge wooden lectern with a row of American flags at his back, casting his eyes to a crowd that stretched far into the Chicago night.

"It's been a long time coming," the president-elect added, "but tonight, because of what we did on this date in this election at this defining moment, change has come to America."

Mr. McCain delivered his concession speech under clear skies on the lush lawn of the Arizona Biltmore, in Phoenix, where he and his wife had held their wedding reception.

The crowd reacted with scattered boos as he offered his congratulations to Mr. Obama and saluted the historical significance of the moment.

"This is a historic election, and I recognize the significance it has for African-Americans and for the special pride that must be theirs tonight," Mr. McCain said, adding, "We both realize that we have come a long way from the injustices that once stained our nation's reputation."

Not only did Mr. Obama capture the presidency, but he led his party to sharp gains in Congress. This puts Democrats in control of the House, the Senate and the White House for the first time since 1995, when Bill Clinton was in office.

The day shimmered with history as voters began lining up before dawn, hours before polls opened, to take part in the culmination of a campaign that over the course of two years commanded an extraordinary amount of attention from the American public.

As the returns became known, and Mr. Obama passed milestone after milestone—Ohio, Florida, Virginia, Pennsylvania, New Hampshire, Iowa and New Mexico—people rolled spontaneously into the streets to celebrate what many described, with perhaps overstated if understandable exhilaration, a new era in a country where just 143 years ago, Mr. Obama, as a black man, could have been owned as a slave.

For Republicans, especially the conservatives who have dominated the party for nearly three decades, the night represented a bitter setback and left them contemplating where they now stand in American politics.

Mr. Obama and his expanded Democratic majority on Capitol Hill now face the task of governing the country through a difficult period: the likelihood of a deep and prolonged recession, and two wars. He took note of those circumstances in a speech that was notable for its sobriety and its absence of the triumphalism that he might understandably have displayed on a night when he won an Electoral College landslide.

"The road ahead will be long, our climb will be steep," said Mr. Obama, his audience hushed and attentive, with some, including the Rev. Jesse Jackson, wiping tears from their eyes. "We may not get there in one year or even one term, but America, I have never been more hopeful than I am tonight that we will get there. I promise you, we as a people will get there." The roster of defeated Republicans included some notable party moderates, like Senator John E. Sununu of New Hampshire and Representative Christopher Shays of Connecticut, and signaled that the Republican conference convening early next year in Washington will be not only smaller but more conservative.

Mr. Obama will come into office after an election in which he laid out a number of clear promises: to cut taxes for most Americans, to get the United States out of Iraq in a fast and orderly fashion, and to expand health care.

In a recognition of the difficult transition

he faces, given the economic crisis, Mr. Obama is expected to begin filling White House jobs as early as this week.

Mr. Obama defeated Mr. McCain in Ohio, a central battleground in American politics, despite a huge effort that brought Mr. McCain and his running mate, Gov. Sarah Palin of Alaska, back there repeatedly. Mr. Obama had lost the state decisively to Senator Hillary Rodham Clinton of New York in the Democratic primary.

Mr. McCain failed to take from Mr. Obama the two Democratic states that were at the top of his target list: New Hampshire and Pennsylvania. Mr. Obama also held on to Minnesota, the state that played host to the convention that nominated Mr. McCain; Wisconsin; and Michigan, a state Mr. McCain once had in his sights.

The apparent breadth of Mr. Obama's sweep left Republicans sobered, and his showing in states like Ohio and Pennsylvania stood out because officials in both parties had said that his struggles there in the primary campaign reflected the resistance of blue-collar voters to supporting a black candidate.

"I always thought there was a potential prejudice factor in the state," Senator Bob Casey, a Democrat of Pennsylvania who was an early Obama supporter, told reporters in Chicago. "I hope this means we washed that away."

Mr. McCain called Mr. Obama at 10 p.m., Central time, to offer his congratulations. In the call, Mr. Obama said he was eager to sit down and talk; in his concession speech, Mr. McCain said he was ready to help Mr. Obama work through difficult times.

"I need your help," Mr. Obama told his rival, according to an Obama adviser, Robert Gibbs. "You're a leader on so many important issues."

Mr. Bush called Mr. Obama shortly after 10 p.m. to congratulate him on his victory.

"I promise to make this a smooth transition," the president said to Mr. Obama, according to a transcript provided by the White House. "You are about to go on one of the great journeys of life. Congratulations, and go enjoy yourself."

For most Americans, the news of Mr. Obama's election came at 11 p.m., Eastern time, when the networks, waiting for the close of polls in California, declared him the victor. A roar sounded from the 125,000 people gathered in Hutchison Field in Grant Park at the moment that they learned Mr. Obama had been projected the winner.

The scene in Phoenix was decidedly more sour. At several points, Mr. McCain, unsmiling, had to motion his crowd to quiet down—he held out both hands, palms down—when they responded to his words of tribute to Mr. Obama with boos.

Mr. Obama, who watched Mr. McCain's speech from his hotel room in Chicago, offered a hand to voters who had not supported him in this election, when he took the stage 15 minutes later. "To those Americans whose support I have yet to earn," he said, "I may not have won your vote, but I hear your voices, I need your help, and I will be your president, too."

Initial signs were that Mr. Obama benefited from a huge turnout of voters, but particularly among blacks. That group made up 13 percent of the electorate, according to surveys of people leaving the polls, compared with 11 percent in 2006.

In North Carolina, Republicans said that the huge surge of African-Americans was one of the big factors that led to Senator Elizabeth Dole, a Republican, losing her re-election bid.

Mr. Obama also did strikingly well among Hispanic voters; Mr. McCain did worse among those voters than Mr. Bush did in 2004. That suggests the damage the Republican Party has suffered among those voters over four years in which Republicans have been at the forefront on the effort to crack down on illegal immigrants.

The election ended what by any definition was one of the most remarkable contests in American political history, drawing what was by every appearance unparalleled public interest.

Throughout the day, people lined up at the polls for hours—some showing up before dawn—to cast their votes. Aides to both campaigns said that anecdotal evidence suggested record-high voter turnout.

Reflecting the intensity of the two candidates, Mr. McCain and Mr. Obama took a page from what Mr. Bush did in 2004 and continued to campaign after the polls opened.

Mr. McCain left his home in Arizona after voting early Tuesday to fly to Colorado

and New Mexico, two states where Mr. Bush won four years ago but where Mr. Obama waged a spirited battle.

These were symbolically appropriate final campaign stops for Mr. McCain, reflecting the imperative he felt of trying to defend Republican states against a challenge from Mr. Obama.

"Get out there and vote," Mr. McCain said in Grand Junction, Colo. "I need your help. Volunteer, knock on doors, get your neighbors to the polls, drag them there if you need to."

By contrast, Mr. Obama flew from his home in Chicago to Indiana, a state that in many ways came to epitomize the audacity of his effort this year. Indiana has not voted for a Democrat since President Lyndon B. Johnson's landslide victory in 1964, and Mr. Obama made an intense bid for support there. He later returned home to Chicago to play basketball, his election-day ritual.

HIGH COURT BANS SCHOOL SEGREGATION; 9-TO-0 DECISION GRANTS TIME TO COMPLY
By Luther A. Huston

Washington, May 17, 1954—The Supreme Court unanimously outlawed today racial segregation in public schools.

Chief Justice Earl Warren read two opinions that put the stamp of unconstitutionality on school systems in twenty-one states and the

District of Columbia where segregation is permissive or mandatory.

The court, taking cognizance of the problems involved in the integration of the school systems concerned, put over until the next term, beginning October, the formulation of decrees to effectuate its 9-to-0 decision.

The opinions set aside the "separate but equal" doctrine laid down by the Supreme Court in 1896.

"In the field of public education," Chief Justice Warren said, "the doctrine of 'separate but equal' has no place. Separate educational facilities are inherently unequal."

He stated the question and supplied the answer as follows:

"We come then to the question presented: Does segregation of children in public schools solely on the basis of race, even though physical facilities and other 'tangible' factors may be equal, deprive the children of the minority group of equal educational opportunities? We believe that it does."

The court's opinion does not apply to private schools. It is directed entirely at public schools. It does not affect the "separate but equal doctrine" as applied on railroads and other public carriers entirely within states that have such restrictions.

The principal ruling of the court was in four cases involving state laws. The states' right to operate separated schools had been argued before the court on two occasions by representatives of South Carolina, Virginia, Kansas and Delaware.

In these cases, consolidated in one opinion, the high court held that school segregation deprived Negroes of "the equal protection of the laws guaranteed by the Fourteenth Amendment."

The other opinion involved the District of Columbia. Here schools have been segregated since Civil War days under laws passed by Congress.

"In view of our decision that the Constitution prohibits the states from maintaining racially segregated public schools," the Chief Justice said, "it would be unthinkable that the same Constitution would impose a lesser duty on the Federal Government.

"We hold that racial segregation in the public schools of the District of Columbia is a denial of the due process of law guaranteed by the Fifth Amendment to the Constitution."

The Fourteenth Amendment provides that no state shall "deny to any person within its jurisdiction the equal protection of the laws." The Fifth Amendment says that no person shall be "deprived of life, liberty or property without due process of law."

The seventeen states having mandatory segregation are Alabama, Arkansas, Delaware, Florida, Mississippi, Missouri, North Carolina, Oklahoma, Georgia, Kentucky, Louisiana, Maryland, South Carolina, Tennessee, Texas, Virginia and West Virginia.

Kansas, New Mexico, Arizona and

Wyoming have permissive statutes, although Wyoming never has exercised it.

South Carolina and Georgia have announced plans to abolish public schools if segregation were banned.

Although the decision with regard to the constitutionality of school segregation was unequivocal, the court set the cases down for reargument in the fall on questions that previously were argued last December. These deal with the power of the court to permit an effective gradual readjustment to school systems not based on color distinctions.

Other questions include whether the court itself should formulate detailed decrees and what issues should be dealt with. Also whether the cases should be remanded to the lower courts to frame decrees, and what general directions the Supreme Court should give the lesser tribunals if this were done.

The cases first came to the high court in 1952 on appeal from rulings of lower Federal courts, handed down in 1951 and 1952. Arguments were heard on Dec. 9–10, 1952.

Unable to reach a decision, the Supreme Court ordered rearguments in the present term and heard the cases for the second time on Dec. 7–8 last year.

Since then, each decision day has seen the courtroom packed with spectators awaiting the ruling. That was true today, though none except the justices themselves knew it was coming down. Reporters were told before the court convened that it "looked like a quiet day."

Three minor opinions had been announced, and those in the press room had begun to believe the prophesy when Banning E. Whittington, the court's press information officer, started putting on his coat.

"Reading of the segregation decisions is about to begin in the court room," he said. "You will get the opinions up there."

The courtroom is one floor up, reached by a long flight of marble steps. Mr. Whittington led a fast moving exodus. In the court room, Chief Justice Warren had just begun reading.

Each of the Associate Justices listened intently. They obviously were aware that no court since the Dred Scott decision of March 6, 1857, had ruled on so vital an issue in the field of racial relations.

Dred Scott was a slave who sued for his freedom on the ground that he had lived in a territory where slavery was forbidden. The territory was the northern part of the Louisiana Purchase, from which slavery was excluded under the terms of the Missouri Compromise.

The Supreme Court ruled that Dred Scott was not a citizen who had a right to sue in the Federal courts, and that Congress had no constitutional power to pass the Missouri Compromise.

Thurgood Marshall, the lawyer who led the fight for racial equality in the public schools, predicted that there would be no disorder and no organized resistance to the Supreme Court's dictum.

He said that the people of the South, the region most heavily affected, were law-abiding and would not "resist the Supreme Court."

Mr. Marshall said that the state presidents of the National Association for the Advancement of Colored People would meet next week-end in Atlanta to discuss further procedures.

The Supreme Court adopted two of the major premises advanced by the Negroes in briefs and arguments presented in support of their cases.

Their main thesis was that segregation, of itself, was unconstitutional. The Fourteenth Amendment, which was adopted July 28, 1868, was intended to wipe out the last vestige of inequality between the races, the Negro side argued.

Against this, lawyers representing the states argued that since there was no specific constitutional prohibition against segregation in the schools, it was a matter for the states, under their police powers, to decide.

The Supreme Court rejected the "states rights" doctrine, however, and found all laws ordering or permitting segregation in the schools to be in conflict with the Federal Constitution.

The Negroes also asserted that segregation had a psychological effect on pupils of the Negro race and was detrimental to the educational system as a whole. The court agreed.

"Today, education is perhaps the most important function of state and local governments," Chief Justice Warren wrote. "Compulsory school attendance laws and the great expenditures for education both demonstrate our recognition of the importance of education in our democratic society. It is the very foundation of good citizenship.

"In these days it is doubtful that any child may reasonably be expected to succeed in life if he is denied the opportunity of an education. Such an opportunity, where the state has undertaken to provide it, must be made available to all on equal terms."

As to the psychological factor, the high court adopted the language of a Kansas court in which the lower bench held:

"Segregation with the sanction of the law, therefore, has a tendency to retard the educational and mental development of Negro children and to deprive them of some of the benefits they would receive in a racially integrated school system."

The "separate but equal" doctrine, demolished by the Supreme Court today, involved transportation, not education. It was the case of Plessy vs. Ferguson, decided in 1896. The court then held that segregation was not unconstitutional if equal facilities were provided for each race.

Since that ruling six cases have been before the Supreme Court, applying the doctrine to public education. In several cases, the court has ordered the admission to colleges and universities of Negro students on the ground that equal facilities were not available in segregated institutions.

Today, however, the court held the doctrine inapplicable under any circumstances to public education.

This means that the court may extend its ruling from primary and secondary schools to include state-supported colleges and universities. Two cases involving Negroes who wish to enter white colleges in Texas and Florida are pending before the court.

The question of "due process," also a clause in the Fourteenth Amendment, had been raised in connection with the state cases as well as the District of Columbia.

The High Court held, however, that since it had ruled in the state cases that segregation was unconstitutional under the "equal protection" clause, it was unnecessary to discuss "whether such segregation also violates the due process clause of the Fourteenth Amendment."

However, the "due process" clause of the Fifth Amendment was the core of the ruling in the District of Columbia case. "Equal protection" and "due process," the court noted, were not always interchangeable phrases.

"Liberty under law extends to the full range of conduct which an individual is free to pursue, and it cannot be restricted except for a proper governmental objective," Chief Justice Warren asserted.

"Segregation in public education is not reasonably related to any proper governmental objective, and thus it imposes on Negro children of the District of Columbia a burden that constitutes an arbitrary deprivation of their liberty in violation of the due process clause."

Two principal surprises attended the announcement of the decision. One was its unanimity. There had been reports that the court was sharply divided and might not be able to get an agreement this term. Very few major rulings of the court have been unanimous.

The second was the appearance with his colleagues of Justice Robert H. Jackson. He suffered a mild heart attack on March 30. He left the hospital last week-end and had not been expected to return to the bench this term, which will end on June 7.

Perhaps to emphasize the unanimity of the court, perhaps from a desire to be present when the history-making verdict was announced, Justice Jackson was in his accustomed seat when the court convened.

NEGRO SITDOWNS STIR FEAR OF WIDER UNREST IN SOUTH
By Claude Sitton

Charlotte, N. C., Feb. 14, 1960—Negro student demonstrations against segregated eating facilities have raised grave questions in the South over the future of the region's race relations. A sounding of opinion in the affected areas showed that much more might be involved than the matter of the Negro's right to sit at a lunch counter for a coffee break.

The demonstrations were generally dismissed at first as another college fad of the "panty-raid" variety. This opinion lost adherents, however, as the movement spread from North Carolina to Virginia, Florida, South Carolina and Tennessee and involved fifteen cities.

Some whites wrote off the episodes as the work of "outside agitators." But even they conceded that the seeds of dissent had fallen in fertile soil.

Appeals from white leaders to leaders in the Negro community to halt the demonstrations bore little fruit. Instead of the hoped-for statements of disapproval, many Negro professionals expressed support for the demonstrators.

A handful of white students joined the protests. And several state organizations endorsed it. Among them were the North Carolina Council on Human Relations, an inter-racial group, and the Unitarian Fellowship for Social Justice, which currently has an all-white membership.

Students of race relations in the area contended that the movement reflected growing dissatisfaction over the slow pace of desegregation in schools and other public facilities.

It demonstrated, they said, a determination to wipe out the last vestiges of segregation.

Moreover, these persons saw a shift of leadership to younger, more militant Negroes. This, they said, is likely to bring increasing use of passive resistance. The technique was conceived by Mohandas K. Gandhi of India and popularized among Southern Negroes by the Rev. Dr. Martin Luther King Jr. He led the bus boycott in Montgomery, Ala. He now heads the Southern Christian Leadership Conference, a Negro minister's group, which seeks to end discrimination.

Negro leaders said that this assessment was correct. They disputed the argument heard among some whites that there was no broad support for the demonstrations outside such organizations as the National Association for the Advancement of Colored People.

There was general agreement on all sides that a sustained attempt to achieve desegregation now, particularly in the Deep South, might breed racial conflict that the region's expanding economy could ill afford.

The spark that touched off the protests was provided by four freshmen at North Carolina Agricultural and Technical College in Greensboro. Even Negroes class Greensboro as one of the most progressive cities in the South in terms of race relations.

On Sunday night, Jan. 31, one of the students sat thinking about discrimination.

"Segregation makes me feel that I'm unwanted," Joseph A. Mc Neil said later in an interview. "I don't want my children exposed to it."

The 17-year-old student from Wilmington, N. C., said that he approached three of his classmates the next morning and found them enthusiastic over a proposal that they demand service at the lunch counter of a downtown variety store.

About 4:45 P.M. they entered the F. W. Woolworth Company store on North Elm Street in the heart of Greensboro. Mr. Joseph said he bought a tube of tooth paste and the others made similar purchases. Then they sat down at the lunch counter.

A Negro woman kitchen helper walked up, according to the students, and told them, "You know you're not supposed to be in here." She later called them "ignorant" and a "disgrace" to their race.

The students then asked a white waitress for coffee.

"I'm sorry but we don't serve colored here," they quoted her.

"I beg your pardon," said Franklin Mc-Cain, 18, of Washington, "you just served me at a counter two feet away. Why is it that you serve me at one counter and deny me at another? Why not stop serving me at all the counters?"

The four students sat, coffee-less, until the store closed at 5:30 P.M. Then, hearing that they might be prosecuted, they went to the executive committee of the Greensboro N.A.A.C.P. to ask advice.

"This was our first knowledge of the demonstration," said Dr. George C. Simkins, who is president of the organization. He said that he had then written to the New York headquarters of the Congress of Racial Equality, which is known as CORE. He requested assistance for the demonstrators, who numbered in the hundreds during the following days.

Dr. Simkins, a dentist, explained that he had heard of a successful attempt, led by CORE, to desegregate a Baltimore restaurant and had read one of the organization's pamphlets.

CORE's field secretary, Gordon R. Carey, arrived from New York on Feb. 7. He said that he had assisted Negro students in some North Carolina cities after they had initiated the protests.

The Greensboro demonstrations and the others that it triggered were spontaneous, according to Mr. Carey. All of the Negroes questioned agreed on this.

The movement's chief targets were two national variety chains, S. H. Kress &, Co. and the F. W. Woolworth Company. Other chains were affected. In some cities the students demonstrated at local stores.

The protests generally followed similar patterns. Young men and women and, in one case, high school boys and girls, walked into the stores and requested food service. Met with refusals in all cases, they remained at the lunch counters in silent protest.

The reaction of store managers in those instances was to close down the lunch counters and, when trouble developed or bomb threats were received, the entire store.

Hastily painted signs, posted on the counters, read: "Temporarily Closed," "Closed for

Repairs," "Closed in the Interest of Public Safety," "No Trespassing," and "We Reserve the Right to Service the Public as We See Fit."

After a number of establishments had shut down in High Point, N. C., the S. H. Kress & Co. store remained open, its lunch counter desegregated. The secret? No stools.

Asked how long the store had been serving all comers on a stand-up basis, the manager replied:

"I don't know. I just got transferred from Mississippi."

The demonstrations attracted crowds of whites. At first the hecklers were youths with duck-tailed haircuts. Some carried small Confederate battle flags. Later they were joined by older men in faded khakis and overalls.

The Negro youths were challenged to step outside and fight. Some of the remarks to the girls were jesting in nature, such as, "How about a date when we integrate?" Other remarks were not.

In a few cases the Negroes were elbowed, jostled and shoved. Itching powder was sprinkled on them and they were spattered with eggs.

At Rock Hill, S. C., a Negro youth was knocked from a stool by a white beside whom he sat. A bottle of ammonia was hurled through the door of a drug store there. The fumes brought tears to the eyes of the demonstrators.

The only arrests reported involved forty-three of the demonstrators. They were seized on a sidewalk outside a Woolworth store at Raleigh shopping center. Charged with trespassing, they posted $50 bonds and were released.

The management of the shopping center contended that the sidewalk was private property.

In most cases, the demonstrators sat or stood at store counters talking in low voices, studying or staring impassively at their tormentors. There was little joking or smiling. Now and then a girl giggled nervously. Some carried Bibles.

Those at Rock Hill were described by the local newspaper, The Evening Herald, as "orderly, polite, well-dressed and quiet."

Questions to their leaders about the reasons for the demonstrations drew such replies as:

"We feel if we can spend our money on other goods we should be able to eat in the same establishments," "All I want is to come in and place my order and be served and leave a tip if I feel like it," and "This is definitely our purpose: integrated seating facilities with no isolated spots, no certain seats, but to sit wherever there is a vacancy."

Some newspapers noted the embarrassing position in which the variety chains found themselves. The News and Observer of Raleigh remarked editorially that in these stores the Negro was a guest, who was cordially invited to the house but definitely not to the table. "And to say the least, this was complicated hospitality."

The newspaper said that to serve the Negroes might offend Southern whites while to do otherwise might result in the loss of the Negro trade.

"This business," it went on, "is causing headaches in New York and irritations in North Carolina. And somehow it revolves around the old saying that you can't have your chocolate cake and eat it too."

The Greensboro Daily news advocated that the lunch counters be closed or else opened on a desegregated basis.

North Carolina's Attorney General, Malcom B. Seawell, asserted that the students were causing "irreparable harm" to relations between whites and Negroes.

Mayor William G. Enloe of Raleigh termed it "regrettable that some of our young Negro students would risk endangering these relations by seeking to change a long-standing custom in a manner that is all but destined to fail."

Some North Carolinians found it incomprehensible that the demonstrations were taking place in their state. They pointed to the progress made here toward desegregation of public facilities. A number of the larger cities in the Piedmont region, among them Greensboro, voluntarily accepted token desegregation of their schools after the Supreme Court's 1954 decisions.

But across the state there were indications that the Negro had weighed token desegregation and found it wanting.

When commenting on the subject, the Rev. F. L. Shuttlesworth of Birmingham, Ala., drew a chorus of "amens" from a packed N.A.A.C.P. meeting in a Greensboro church, "We don't want token freedom," he declared. "We want full freedom. What would a token dollar be worth?"

Warming to the subject, he shouted:

"You educated us. You taught us to look up, white man. And we're looking up!"

Praising the demonstrators, he urged his listeners to be ready "to go to jail with Jesus" if necessary to "remove the dead albatross of segregation that makes America stink in the eyes of the world."

John H. Wheeler, a Negro lawyer who heads a Durham bank, said that the only difference among Negroes concerned the "when" and "how" of the attack on segregation.

He contended that the question was whether the South would grant the minority race full citizenship status or commit economic suicide by refusing to do so.

The Durham Committee on Negro Affairs, which includes persons from many economic levels, pointed out in a statement that white officials had asked Negro leaders to stop the student demonstrations.

"It is our opinion," the statement said, "that instead of expressing disapproval, we have an obligation to support any peaceful movement which seeks to remove from the customs of our beloved Southland those unfair practices based upon race and color which have for so long a time been recognized as a stigma on our way of life and stumbling block to social and economic progress of the region."

It then asserted:

"It is reasonable to expect that our state officials will recognize their responsibility for helping North Carolina live up to its reputation of being the enlightened, liberal and progressive state, which our industry hunters have been representing it to be."

The outlook for not only this state but also for the entire region is for increasing Negro resistance to segregation, according to Harold C. Fleming, executive director of the Southern Regional Council. The council is an interracial group of Southern leaders with headquarters in Atlanta. Its stated aim is the improvement of race relations.

"The lunch-counter 'sit-in'," Mr. Fleming commented, "demonstrates something that the white community has been reluctant to face: the mounting determination of Negroes to be rid of all segregated barriers.

"Those who hoped that token legal adjustments to school desegregation would dispose of the racial issues are on notice to the contrary. We may expect more, not less, protests of this kind against enforced segregation in public facilities and services of all types."

2 NEGRO STUDENTS ENTER GEORGIA U.

By Claude Sitton

ATHENS, Ga., Jan. 10, 1961—Two Negroes enrolled in the University of Georgia today after Gov. S. Ernest Vandiver Jr. had been enjoined from cutting off funds and forcing the school to close.

Some 2,000 white students ringed the Academic Building while the two paid their tuition fees, thus completing registration and becoming full-fledged students at the university. There were several outbursts of jeering and segregationist chanting, and a few youths milled excitedly around the Negroes when they emerged. There was no violence.

The admission of Charlayne Alberta Hunter, 18 years old, and Hamilton E. Holmes, 19, both of Atlanta, marked the first desegregation at any level in the state's public education system. Shortly after they registered, the United States Supreme Court denied a plea to delay integration.

About 400 students massed at 9 o'clock tonight outside the girls' dormitory in a demonstration that lasted for two hours. A majority appeared to be merely curious.

But some youths set off fireworks and chanted vulgar anti-integration slogans. A cameraman was knocked to the sidewalk, cutting his face and breaking his glasses. Coffee was tossed on two other cameramen. A large rock hurled at a group of newsmen struck a co-ed on the leg. Fire crackers and several eggs were thrown at passing cars.

University officials praised the girls in the dormitory. They said that many of the students had spoken to Miss Hunter and welcomed her to the campus. Judge William A. Bootle made the entry of the two Negroes possible by granting an injunction against Governor Vandiver this morning in Federal District Court at Macon. The jurist had handed down the original desegregation order. Yesterday he stayed the order, only to see it reinstated by an Appellate judge.

Mr. Vandiver was forbidden today to invoke a provision of the state appropriation act to cut off funds to the school. The provision makes it illegal for state aid to be continued to a university that has been desegregated by a Federal Court.

The Governor had announced early today that he would shut off the school's funds if the Negroes completed registration. University officials had planned to declare the rest of the week a holiday while the Legislature took action to repeal the law.

Meanwhile, Eugene Cook, the state Attorney General, and B.D. Murphy, special counsel for the state in the case, flew to Washington to request a delay of desegregation pending an appeal. The request was rejected unanimously by the Supreme Court.

Leaders of the Legislature, meeting for the second day in their current session in Atlanta, generally expressed relief at Judge Bootle's ruling. Most of them had indicated opposition to any action that might close the university, although it was conceded that Governor Vandiver had no choice but to shut off its funds.

Governor Vandiver, in a telegram to Judge Bootle, ruled out the possibility of any act of defiance. But he protested against what he termed "your action of interference in the administration of state law and what amounts to usurpation of the legislative prerogatives of the General Assembly of Georgia."

The Governor termed false certain widespread reports that he had already halted state aid to the school.

"It is a shocking circumstance when judicial orders are issued in this fashion based upon newspaper reports and affidavits of plaintiffs' attorneys," he said.

Miss Hunter and Mr. Holmes left Atlanta by car for Athens, some seventy miles northeast of the state capital, shortly after noon, when word of the judge's action reached them. They were accompanied by Mrs. Althea Hunter, the girl's mother, and a lawyer and several friends. The group entered the registrar's office at 2:25 P.M. through a side entrance while some 800 to 1,000 students waited at an entrance to the campus on the other side of the building.

Some of the students rushed into the hallway after learning that the Negroes had arrived. They chanted, "Two, four, six, eight, we don't want to integrate."

Paul R. Kea, assistant director of admissions, ordered the hall cleared after the students ignored his warning to remain quiet. The final act of registration—and the desegregation of the 175-year-old university and its all-white student body of more than 7,200—took place after the Negroes walked into the treasurer's office at 3:12 P.M. There they paid a tuition fee of $65 each plus an $11 fee for late registration, standard procedure in such cases.

Miss Hunter is being housed in a private room at Myers Hall. The room has its own cooking and bathing facilities. However, she is expected to eat in the student cafeteria. Mr. Holmes obtained a room in town because of a lack of dormitory space. He is expected to move on to the campus in several months.

Dr. O. C. Aderhold, the university president, issued late today a statement praising the student body for its "good judgment and conduct." The campus had been in a state of confusion as a result of the report that the Governor had closed the institution. Many students stayed away from classes today.

More than 1,000 youths staged a raucous, sometimes disorderly, parade last night through downtown Athens behind a Confederate flag. Dean of Men William Tate and the city police put down the demonstration with some difficulty. University officials expressed confidence today that there would be no repetition of the cross-burning, marching and segregationist chanting that had marked student gatherings in the last few days.

400 U.S. MARSHALS SENT TO ALABAMA AS MONTGOMERY BUS RIOTS HURT 20; PRESIDENT BIDS STATE KEEP ORDER
By Anthony Lewis

Washington, May 20, 1961—The Federal Government dispatched 400 marshals and other armed officers to Alabama tonight to restore order in areas that were torn by racial violence.

The Government acted after a mob of white persons attacked a racially mixed group of bus riders in Montgomery, Ala. The disorders lasted two hours. At least twenty of the riders were beaten.

Attorney General Robert F. Kennedy announced the Federal action in a telegram to Alabama officials. He said it was necessary to "guarantee safe passage in interstate commerce."

The 400 Federal marshals will be in Montgomery by noon tomorrow, a Justice Department spokesman said. He said they would have arm bands for identification and would carry sidearms as well as tear-gas bombs and riot clubs or night sticks.

Mr. Kennedy disclosed also that he would ask the Federal Court in Montgomery "to enjoin the Ku Klux Klan, the National States Rights Party, certain individuals and all persons acting in concert with them from interfering with peaceful interstate travel by buses."

A Justice Department spokesman said that there were reports of Ku Klux Klan and Negro groups converging on Montgomery County and that he was afraid of larger scale problems than had already developed.

The Attorney General acted immediately after President Kennedy issued a statement deploring the mob attacks.

The President said the situation in

Alabama was "a source of the deepest concern to me as it must be to the vast majority of the citizens of Alabama and all Americans."

"I have instructed the Justice Department to take all necessary steps," the President added.

He called on Gov. John Patterson of Alabama and other state and local officials "to exercise their lawful authority to prevent any further outbreaks of violence."

"I hope that state and local officials in Alabama will meet their responsibilities," the President said. "The United States Government intends to meet its."

The President said he hoped that all persons, whether citizens of Alabama or visitors, "would refrain from any action which would in any way tend to provoke further outbreaks." His brother, the Attorney General, said that this was not intended as a suggestion to the bus riders that they give up their trip, but was a general appeal for restraint.

The Justice Department said that it was sending marshals and specially deputized marshals to Montgomery from nearby areas and from the District of Columbia.

They are already on the way by air and automobile, a spokesman for the Justice Department said.

Byron R. White, the Deputy Attorney General, went to Montgomery to take charge of the operation there.

Justice Department officials emphasized that no members of the armed forces were being sent.

This was in contrast to the action of President Eisenhower in 1957. Paratroopers were sent then to end violence over school desegregation in Little Rock, Ark.

The marshals were dispatched to Alabama under authority of an 1871 statute which also had been the legal basis for the sending of troops to Little Rock.

The statute says that the President may use "the militia or the armed forces . . . or any other means . . . to suppress in a state any insurrection, domestic violence, unlawful combination or conspiracy" under certain specified conditions.

These conditions are that a class of citizens is deprived of a constitutional right "and the constituted authorities of that state are unable, fail, or refuse to protect that right."

Robert Kennedy announced his action in a telegram sent to the Alabama public safety director, Floyd Mann, and the Mayors of Birmingham and Montgomery, besides Governor Patterson.

In the telegram Mr. Kennedy reviewed discussions that he and other Justice Department officials had had with the Governor and his aides since Monday about "this very explosive situation."

He noted that just last night his own administrative assistant, John Seigenthaler, had met with the Governor and had been given the assurance that the state government had "The will, the force, the men and the equipment to fully protect everyone in Alabama."

He added that the Governor had suggested the Justice Department notify the Greyhound Bus Company that a guarantee of safety had been given by the state.

"It was based on his assurance of safe conduct," the Attorney General telegraphed Governor Patterson, "that the students boarded the bus in Birmingham on their trip to Montgomery. These students boarded the bus this morning. They arrived in Montgomery and were attacked and beaten by a mob."

The suit that Mr. Kennedy said was being brought to enjoin interference with interstate travel was a most unusual legal step.

Ordinarily the Justice Department cannot bring an injunction suit unless there is a specific statute authorizing it to do so, and there is none here.

However, in 1895, in the landmark case of In re Debs, the Supreme Court held that the Federal Government had inherent authority to go to the courts to break up any violence interfering with interstate commerce.

The issue at that time was a railroad strike that had shut off the mails. The United States got an injunction against the strike and then prosecuted some of the strike leaders, including the Socialist Eugene V. Debs for contempt of the injunction. The Supreme Court upheld the contempt prosecution.

The Debs case stands as a rarity in American legal history. A Justice Department authority said today that it was on the basis of the Debs ruling that the department was asserting the power to go into the Federal courts and enjoin individuals and organizations in Alabama from interfering with interstate travel.

The Government's moves this evening were planned at a meeting that lasted all afternoon in the Attorney General's office. President Kennedy, who flew to his country home in Middleburg, Va., in mid-afternoon, kept in touch with his brother by telephone.

Attorney General Kennedy was called into his office from an F.B.I. baseball game where he was throwing out the first ball. He was in shirtsleeves and still wearing a baseball cap as he conferred on the critical situation in Alabama.

In the conference were virtually all the top advisers except those who happened to be out of town.

They included Mr. White and three of his assistants, Joseph F. Dolan, William A. Geoghegan and Clive W. Palmer.

Three assistant attorneys general were in the conference—Burke Marshall of the Civil Rights Division, Herbert J. Miller of the Criminal Division and Louis F. Oberdorfer of the Tax Division.

Representing the office of legal counsel was Harold F. Reiff.

From the Attorney General's personal staff were his executive assistant, Andrew F. Cehmann; the chief of public information, Edwin O. Guthmann and David Hackett.

3,000 TROOPS PUT DOWN MISSISSIPPI RIOTING AND SEIZE 200 AS NEGRO ATTENDS CLASSES

By Claude Sitton

OXFORD, Miss., Oct. 1, 1962—James H. Meredith, a Negro, enrolled in the University of Mississippi today and began classes as Federal troops and federalized units of the Mississippi National Guard quelled a 15-hour riot.

A force of more than 3,000 soldiers and guardsmen and 400 deputy United States marshals fired rifles and hurled tear-gas grenades to stop the violent demonstrations.

Throughout the day more troops streamed into Oxford. Tonight a force approaching 5,000 soldiers and guardsmen, along with the Federal marshals, maintained an uneasy peace in this town of 6,500 in the northern Mississippi hills.

[There were two flareups tonight in which tear gas had to be used, United Press International reported. A small crowd of students began throwing bottles at marshals outside Baxter Hall where Mr. Meredith was housed. They were quickly dispersed by tear gas. Soldiers also broke up a minor demonstration at a downtown intersection.]

The troops seized approximately 200 persons.

They were seated in the mobs of students and adults that besieged the university administration building last night and attacked troops on the town square this morning.

Among those arrested was former Maj. Gen. Edwin A. Walker, who resigned his commission after having been reprimanded for his ultra-right-wing political activity. He was charged with insurrection.

The university's acceptance of Mr. Meredith, a 29-year-old Air Force veteran, followed Gov. Ross R. Barnett's retreat from his defiance of Federal court orders that the Negro be enrolled.

The 64-year-old official, a member of the militantly segregationist citizens Councils, had vowed he would go to jail if necessary to prevent university desegregation.

Mr. Meredith's admission marked the first desegregation of a public educational institution in Mississippi. It reduced the Deep South bloc of massive-resistance states to two—Alabama and South Carolina.

Although the step brought an apparent end to the most serious Federal-state conflict since the Civil War, its cost in human lives and bitterness was the greatest in any dispute over desegregation directives of the Federal courts.

Two men were killed in the rioting, which broke out about 8 o'clock last night after Mr. Meredith had been escorted onto the campus by the marshals.

The victims were Paul Guihard, 30 years old, a correspondent for Agence France Presse, and Ray Gunter, 23, a jukebox repairman from nearby Abbeville, Miss.

The number of injured could not be

determined definitely. But Mr. Guthman told newsmen 25 marshals had required medical treatment. One of them, shot through the neck, was reported in critical condition.

A military spokesman said 20 soldiers and guardsmen had been injured, none of them seriously.

Dr. Vernon B. Harrison, director of the Student Health Service, said between 60 and 70 persons, including some marshals, had been treated at the university infirmary.

Others who were wounded or were burned by exploding tear-gas grenades obtained aid from local physicians or from Army doctors who moved into the infirmary last night.

Lieut. Gen. Hamilton Howze, commander of the 18th Airborne Corps, arrived here from Fort Bragg, in North Carolina, to take over the field command. The corps includes the 82d and the 101st Airborne Divisions.

Lieut. Col. Gordon Hill, Army public information officer here, said General Howze was accompanied by his corps command. There were reports that other units of the two famed airborne divisions were moving into the area.

The general's presence indicated that a major build-up of Army troops was under way here, in Columbus, Miss., and at Memphis.

General Howze took over command from Brig. Gen. Charles Billingslea, assistant commander of the Second Infantry Division, Fort Benning, Ga.

Mr. Guthman said Federal forces were prepared to remain as long as necessary.

"Our mission is to see that the orders of the courts are enforced," he said.

Asked if the mission included the preservation of order in the town, he replied: "I think we have a duty to maintain law and order."

The toll of property damaged included five automobiles and a mobile television unit that were burned.

Bricks, lumber and other building materials were stolen from a construction site and used as missiles or roadblocks. The rioters ripped up the garden of a home in their search for brickbats and commandeered a fire engine and a bulldozer.

A hard core of 70 to 100 youths, most of whom appeared to be Ole Miss students, touched off the riot. They were soon joined by students from other universities and colleges in this area.

Youths and men from Lafayette County, of which Oxford is the seat, and from surrounding counties joined the fray.

Some members of the mob wore jackets from Mississippi State University, at Starkeville, and Memphis State College, in Memphis.

Members of the Ku Klux Klan and similar racist groups in Alabama and northern Louisiana reportedly had threatened to join the opposition against Mr. Meredith's enrollment.

In briefing newsmen, Mr. Guthman flatly denied assertions by state officials that Chief United States Marshal James J. P. McShane had precipitated the riot by ordering use of tear gas prematurely.

The Justice Department spokesman said tear gas had been used only after the students had showered the marshals with rocks and one deputy had been struck with an iron pipe, which left a deep dent in his helmet.

A force of 200 state troopers, used by Governor Barnett to block one of Mr. Meredith's three previous attempts to register, stood by on and around the campus last night. The troopers made no effort to break up the mob at the administration building, called the Lyceum. Some made it plain they sided with the students.

The troopers pulled back from the riot scene shortly after 9 o'clock, leaving the marshals to defend themselves.

The action was authorized by State Senator George Yarborough of Red Banks, the President pro tem of the Senate and Governor Barnett's official representative on the campus.

"We had been assured by the Governor that the state police would assist us in maintaining law and order," Mr. Guthman said.

The besieged marshals, commanded by Chief Marshal McShane and Nicholas deB. Katzenbach, Deputy United States Attorney General, held their redoubt at the Lyceum until shortly after midnight.

They got reinforcement then from Troop E. Second Reconnaissance Squadron, 108th Armored Cavalry, of the Mississippi National Guard.

The first unit of combat military policemen

called up by the President did not arrive until 4:30 this morning. This was Company A of the 503d Military Police Battalion, from Fort Bragg, N.C.

Other troops poured into Oxford by truck and by plane. They included the 716th Military Police Battalion, which came overland from Fort Dix, N.J.; the 720th Military Police Battalion from Fort Hood, Tex.; the Second Battle Group, Second Infantry Division, from Fort Benning, Ga.; and the 31st Helicopter Company from Jacksonville, N.C.

The Mississippi National Guard units sent here included the 108th Armored Cavalry Regiment from Tupelo and the Second Battle Group, 155th Infantry, from Amory.

A detachment of the 70th Engineering Battalion from Fort Campbell, Kentucky, operated a "tent city" for the marshals 15 miles north of here, in the Holly Springs National Forest.

The unit included medical and communications specialists from the 101st Airborne Division.

The 101st had been ordered to Little Rock, Ark., in September of 1957 by President Eisenhower to put down rioting and to enforce Federal court desegregation orders directing the admission of nine Negroes to Central High School.

The first military policeman to arrive helped the marshals and National Guardsmen repel a final assault on the Lyceum at 5 A.M. Barrage after barrage of tear gas and smoke grenades drove back the howling mob, whose strength had dwindled from a peak of 2,500 to 100.

It was difficult to estimate the number of persons who actually took part in the riot. Acrid clouds of smoke and tear gas billowed across the front of a campus area called the Grove, a tree-shaded oval in front of the Lyceum.

Virtually all the street lights were shot out or broken by rocks early in the evening. Observers edging as close to the action as the tear gas and prudence would permit got a view of shadowy forms racing back and forth behind Confederate battle flags.

The rioters cranked up the bulldozer twice and sent it crashing driverless toward the marshals. Both times it hit trees and other obstructions that stopped it before it reached their ranks.

Shouting members of the mob raced the fire engine back and forth through the trees and strewed links of hose across the Grove. At one point the engine careened down the asphalt drive only a few feet from the marshals, who peppered it with blasts from their tear-gas guns.

Several persons were burned as canisters of tear gas struck them or exploded near them.

Snipers operated under the cover of darkness, aiming blasts of birdshot and pistol and rifle fire at the marshals and others.

Mr. Guihard received a bullet wound in the back. Mr. Gunter was shot in the forehead.

A sniper fired three quick shots at Karl Fleming, a reporter in the Atlanta bureau of Newsweek magazine, but the bullet struck the doorway of the Lyceum.

Other newsmen were attacked and beaten. Gordon Yoder, a Telenews cameraman from Dallas, and Mrs. Yoder were set upon by the mob. State troopers rescued them.

A group of teen-agers and a few men massed on the town square before the three-story Lafayette County Courthouse about 9:30 A.M. today. Many of them wore gray caps bearing Confederate battle flags.

They took up positions on the southeast corner of the square, facing two platoons of military policemen on the southwest corner. About a third of the M.P.'s were Negroes.

The youths began hurling bottles at the soldiers, drawing lusty cheers from adult bystanders when they scored a hit. The soldiers remained in ranks.

The platoons fixed bayonets, formed two wedges and scattered the assailants. But the mob returned and began tossing bottles and rocks at the soldiers again.

The M.P.'s donned their gas masks, formed in a line and moved across the square, throwing tear-gas grenades. The youths retreated.

The mob returned again, and squads of eight to ten soldiers chased them back along the streets, firing rifles over their heads. This broke up the mob.

Business establishments that had opened this morning closed their doors hurriedly. Except for the troops, the square was deserted at noon.

200,000 MARCH FOR CIVIL RIGHTS IN ORDERLY WASHINGTON RALLY; PRESIDENT SEES GAIN FOR NEGRO

By E. W. KENSWORTHY

Washington, Aug. 28, 1963—More than 200,000 Americans, most of them black but many of them white, demonstrated here today for a full and speedy program of civil rights and equal job opportunities.

It was the greatest assembly for a redress of grievances that this capital has ever seen.

One hundred years and 240 days after Abraham Lincoln enjoined the emancipated slaves to "abstain from all violence" and "labor faithfully for reasonable wages," this vast throng proclaimed in march and song and through the speeches of their leaders that they were still waiting for the freedom and the jobs.

There was no violence to mar the demonstration. In fact, at times there was an air of hootenanny about it as groups of schoolchildren clapped hands and swung into the familiar freedom songs.

But if the crowd was good-natured, the underlying tone was one of dead seriousness. The emphasis was on "freedom" and "now." At the same time the leaders emphasized, paradoxically but realistically, that the struggle was just beginning.

On Capitol Hill, opinion was divided about the impact of the demonstration in stimulating Congressional action on civil rights legislation. But at the White House, President Kennedy declared that the cause of 20,000,000 Negroes had been advanced by the march.

The march leaders went from the shadows of the Lincoln Memorial to the White House to meet with the President for 75 minutes. Afterward, Mr. Kennedy issued a 400-word statement praising the marchers for the "deep fervor and the quiet dignity" that had characterized the demonstration.

The nation, the President said, "can properly be proud of the demonstration that has occurred here today."

The main target of the demonstration was Congress, where committees are now considering the administration's civil rights bill.

At the Lincoln Memorial this afternoon, some speakers, knowing little of the way of Congress, assumed that the passage of a strengthened civil rights bill had been assured by the moving events of the day.

But from statements by Congressional leaders, after they had met with the march committee this morning, this did not seem certain at all. These statements came before the demonstration.

Senator Mike Mansfield, of Montana, the Senate Democratic leader, said he could not say whether the mass protest would speed the legislation, which faces a filibuster by Southerners.

Senator Everett McKinley Dirksen of Illinois, the Republican leader, said he thought the demonstration would be neither an advantage nor a disadvantage to the prospects for the civil rights bill.

The human tide that swept over the Mall between the shrines of Washington and Lincoln fell back faster than it came on. As soon as the ceremony broke up this afternoon, the exodus began. With astounding speed, the last buses and trains cleared the city by midevening.

At 9 P.M. the city was as calm as the waters of the Reflecting Pool between the two memorials.

At the Lincoln Memorial early in the afternoon, in the midst of a songfest before the addresses, Josephine Baker, the singer, who had flown from her home in Paris, said to the thousands stretching down both sides of the Reflecting Pool:

"You are on the eve of a complete victory. You can't go wrong. The world is behind you."

Miss Baker said, as if she saw a dream coming true before her eyes, that "this is the happiest day of my life."

But of all the 10 leaders of the march on Washington who followed her, only the Rev. Dr. Martin Luther King Jr., president of the Southern Christian Leadership Conference, saw that dream so hopefully.

The other leaders, except for the three clergymen among the 10, concentrated on the struggle ahead and spoke in tough, even harsh, language.

But paradoxically it was King—who had suffered perhaps most of all—who ignited the crowd with words that might have been written by the sad, brooding man enshrined within.

As he arose, a great roar welled up from the crowd. When he started to speak, a hush fell.

"Even though we face the difficulties of today and tomorrow, I still have a dream," he said.

"It is a dream that one day this nation will rise up and live out the true meaning of its creed: 'We hold these truths to be self-evident, that all men are created equal.'"

"I have a dream . . ." The vast throng listening intently to him roared.

". . . that one day on the red hills of Georgia, the sons of former slaves and the sons of former slave-owners will be able to sit together at the table of brotherhood.

"I have a dream . . ." The crowd roared.

". . . that one day even the State of Mississippi, a state sweltering with the heat of injustice, sweltering with the heat of oppression, will be transformed into an oasis of freedom and justice.

"I have a dream . . ." The crowd roared.

". . . that my four little children will one day live in a nation where they will not be judged by the color of their skin but by the content of their character.

"I have a dream . . ." The crowd roared.

". . . that one day every valley shall be exalted, every hill and mountain shall be made low, the rough places will be made plain, and the crooked places will be made straight, and the glory of the Lord shall be revealed and all flesh shall see it together."

As Dr. King concluded with a quotation from a Negro hymn—"Free at last, free at last, thank God almighty"—the crowd, recognizing that he was finishing, roared once again and waved their signs and pennants.

But the civil rights leaders, who knew the strength of the forces arrayed against them from past battles, knew also that a hard struggle lay ahead. The tone of their speeches was frequently militant.

Roy Wilkins, executive secretary of the National Association for the Advancement of Colored People, made it plain that he and his colleagues thought the President's civil rights still did not go nearly far enough. He said:

"The President's proposals represent so moderate an approach that if any one is weakened or eliminated, the remainder will be little more than sugar water. Indeed, the package needs strengthening."

Harshest of all the speakers was John Lewis, chairman of the Student Nonviolent Coordinating Committee.

"My friends," he said, "Let us not forget that we are involved in a serious social revolution. But by and large American politics is dominated by politicians who build their career on immoral compromising and ally themselves with open forums of political, economic and social exploitation."

He concluded:

"They're talking about slowdown and stop. We will not stop.

"If we do not get meaningful legislation out of this Congress, the time will come when we will not confine our marching to Washington. We will march through the South, through the streets of Jackson, through the streets of Danville, through the streets of Cambridge, through the streets of Birmingham.

"But we will march with the spirit of love and the spirit of dignity that we have shown here today."

In the original text of the speech, distributed last night, Mr. Lewis said:

"We will not wait for the President, the Justice Department, nor the Congress, but we will take matters into our own hands and create a source of power, outside of any national structure, that could and would assure us a victory."

He also said in the original text that "we will march through the South, through the heart of Dixie, the way Sherman did."

It was understood that at least the last of these statements was changed as a result of a protest by the Most Rev. Patrick J. O'Boyle, Roman Catholic Archbishop of Washington, who refused to give the invocation if the offending words were spoken by Mr. Lewis.

The great day really began the night before. As a half moon rose over the lagoon by the Jefferson Memorial and the tall lighted shaft of the Washington Monument gleamed in the reflecting pool, a file of Negroes from out of town began climbing the steps of the Lincoln Memorial.

There, while the carpenters nailed the last planks on the television platforms for the next day the TV technicians called through the loudspeakers, "Final audio, one, two, three, four," a middle-aged Negro couple, the man's arm around the shoulders of his plump wife, stood and read with their lips:

"If we shall suppose that American slavery is one of the offenses which in the providence of God must needs come, but which having continued through His appointed time, He now wills to remove . . ."

The day dawned clear and cool. At 7 A.M. the town had a Sunday appearance, except for the shuttle buses drawn up in front of Union Station, waiting.

By 10 A.M. there were 40,000 on the slopes around the Washington Monument. An hour later the police estimated the crowd at 90,000. And still they poured in.

Because some things went wrong at the monument, everything was right. Most of the stage and screen celebrities from New York and Hollywood who were scheduled to begin entertaining the crowd at 10 did not arrive at the airport until 11:15.

As a result the whole affair at the monument grounds began to take on the spontaneity of a church picnic. Even before the entertainment was to begin, groups of high school students were singing with wonderful improvisations and hand-clapping all over the monument slope.

Civil rights demonstrators who had been released from jail in Danville, Va., were singing:

"Move on, move on. Till all the world is free."

And members of Local 144 of the Hotel and Allied Service Employees Union from New York City, an integrated local since 1950, were stomping:

"Oh, freedom, we shall not, we shall not be moved, Just like a tree that's planted by the water."

Then the pros took over, starting with the folk singers. The crowd joined in with them.

Joan Baez started things rolling with "the song"—"We Shall Overcome."

"Oh deep in my heart I do believe We shall overcome some day."

And Peter, Paul, and Mary sang "How many times must a man look up before he can see the sky."

And Odetta's great, full-throated voice carried almost to Capitol Hill: "If they ask you who you are, tell them you're a child of God."

Jackie Robinson told the crowd that "we cannot be turned back," and Norman Thomas, the venerable Socialist, said: "I'm glad I lived long enough to see this day."

The march to the Lincoln Memorial was supposed to start at 11:30, behind the leaders. But at 11:20 it set off spontaneously down Constitution Avenue behind the Kenilworth Knights, a local drum and bugle corps dazzling in yellow silk blazers, green trousers and green berets.

Apparently forgotten was the intention to

make the march to the Lincoln Memorial a solemn tribute to Medgar W. Evers, N.A.A.C.P. official murdered in Jackson, Miss., last June 12, and others who had died for the cause of civil rights.

The leaders were lost, and they never did get to the head of the parade.

The leaders included also Walter P. Reuther, head of the United Automobile Workers; A. Philip Randolph, head of the American Negro Labor Council; the Rev. Dr. Eugene Carson Blake, vice chairman of the Commission on Religion and Race of the National Council of Churches; Mathew Ahmann, executive director of the National Catholic Conference for Interracial Justice; Rabbi Joachim Prinz, president of the American Jewish Congress; Whitney M. Young Jr., executive director of the National Urban League; and James Farmer, president of the Congress of Racial Equality.

All spoke at the memorial except Mr. Farmer, who is in jail in Louisiana following his arrest as a result of a civil rights demonstration. His speech was read by Floyd B. McKissick, CORE national chairman.

At the close of the ceremonies at the Lincoln Memorial, Bayard Rustin, the organizer of the march, asked Mr. Randolph, who conceived it, to lead the vast throng in a pledge.

Repeating after Mr. Randolph, the marchers pledged "complete personal commitment to the struggle for jobs and freedom for Americans" and "to carry the message of the march to my friends and neighbors back home and arouse them to an equal commitment and an equal effort."

3 IN RIGHTS DRIVE REPORTED MISSING
By Claude Sitton

Philadelphia, Miss., June 22, 1964—Three workers in a day-old civil rights campaign in Mississippi were reported missing today after their release from jail here last night.

Leaders of the drive said they feared that the three men—two whites, both from New York, and one Negro, had met with foul play.

The three had been held by Neshoba County authorities for four hours following the arrest of one on a speeding charge and the jailing of the others "for investigation."

Agents of the Federal Bureau of Investigation began arriving here in force early tonight after the Justice Department ordered a full-scale search.

The Mississippi Highway Patrol issued a missing-persons bulletin, but a spokesman in Jackson indicated late today that it had no plans at present for further action.

All three missing men arrived in Mississippi late Saturday afternoon from Oxford, Ohio, where they had taken part in a one-week orientation course for the statewide project. They were among the advance group of some 175 workers who are expected to be followed by another 800 participants in the campaign of political action, education and cultural activities among Negroes.

One of the missing whites is Michael Schwerner of Brooklyn, a 24-year-old former settlement-house worker. He came here six months ago with his wife, Rita, to open one of the first community centers for Negroes in Mississippi. Mrs. Schwerner remained at Oxford to take part in the second orientation course for volunteers.

The second missing man is Andrew Goodman, 20, a student volunteer from Queens.

The third is James E. Chaney, 21, a Meridian plasterer and driver of the late-model Ford station wagon in which they were last seen.

Both Mr. Schwerner and Mr. Chaney are members of a civil rights task force organized by the Congress of Racial Equality, which is cooperating with the Student Nonviolent Coordinating Committee and other organizations in the Mississippi project.

Concern over the fate of the three was heightened by the fact that the two CORE men had always reported their whereabouts before at frequent intervals, according to campaign spokesmen in Jackson. Workers in the Meridian drive headquarters said Mr. Schwerner had repeatedly emphasized the importance of this to the others during their drive here from Oxford.

Further, the prospect of the civil rights campaign had led to an increasing number of violent incidents even before the workers began arriving last Friday.

The three men left Meridian yesterday at about 9:30 A.M. for Philadelphia, about 35 miles away, where they planned to look into the burning of the Mount Zion Methodist Church last Tuesday night. The Negro church was in the Longdale community, some 12 miles east of this town of 5,500 persons in east-central Mississippi.

Cecil Price, the Neshoba County deputy sheriff, said he had halted and arrested the three about 5:30 P.M. yesterday. He said Mr. Chaney had been driving 65 miles an hour in a 30-mile zone on the outskirts of Philadelphia before he stopped them. The whites were held "for investigation."

The three were released from the county jail here at 10:30 P.M. after Mr. Chaney paid a $20 fine.

"I told them to leave the country," said Mr. Price. The three then drove out along State Highway 19 after having told the deputy they were returning to Meridian, according to him.

Sheriff L. A. Rainey, a burly, tobacco-chewing man, showed little concern over the report that the workers were missing.

"If they're missing, they just hid somewhere, trying to get a lot of publicity out of it, I figure," he said.

Robert Weil, spokesman for the campaign headquarters in Jackson, said campaign leaders "definitely fear that there was foul play, perhaps by the local citizens after they were released."

Washington, June 22—The Federal Bureau of Investigation has been ordered to make a full inquiry into the disappearance of the three civil rights volunteers.

Edwin O. Guthman, Justice Department spokesman, said:

"We are investigating the possibility that they are being held against their will by persons who are not law-enforcement officers or that they are otherwise being deprived of their civil liberties."

Mr. Guthman also said that the Department of Justice wanted to question the volunteers about the circumstances of their arrest and release.

Headquarters of the Congress of Racial Equality in New York City said yesterday that Michael Schwerner and his wife had been in Mississippi for CORE since last January. They were running a Community Center at Meridian where Negroes were trained for civil service examinations, voter registration and in other phases of the civil rights program.

Before joining CORE, Mr. Schwerner was a group worker at Hamilton-Madison House, a social center at 50 Madison Street on the Lower East Side of Manhattan. He and his wife lived at 364 Henry Street, in Brooklyn Heights.

Mr. Schwerner's parents live in Pelham, in Westchester County. He attended Cornell and Columbia.

Andrew Goodman is an anthropology student at Queens College and lived with his parents, Mr. and Mrs. Robert W. Goodman, at 161 West 86th Street. He had arrived at Meridian only 24 hours before starting out on the trip with Mr. Schwerner and James

Chaney. He was one of the group of Northern volunteers who had been taking instruction at Oxford, Ohio.

Mrs. Goodman is a practicing psychologist and her husband is a civil engineer.

DR. KING LEADS MARCH AT SELMA; STATE POLICE END IT PEACEABLY UNDER A U.S.-ARRANGED ACCORD
By Roy Reed

SELMA, Ala., March 9, 1965—The Rev. Dr. Martin Luther King Jr. led 1,500 Negroes and whites on a second attempted protest march today. State troopers turned them back on the outskirts of Selma, after they had gone one mile.

But this time there was no violence— unlike a similar confrontation at the same spot on Sunday. Then, troopers and Dallas County sheriff's officers broke up an attempted march to Montgomery, the state capital, 50 miles away, with clubs and tear gas.

"We had the greatest demonstration for freedom today that we've ever had in the South," Dr. King said as he disbanded the brief march today.

Tonight, three Unitarian ministers who had participated in the march were beaten by whites on a downtown street corner. The ministers are white.

One of them, the Rev. James J. Reeb, 38 years old, of Boston, was taken to University Hospital in Birmingham with a serious head injury and later underwent surgery. The police said he had been knocked unconscious with a club.

The Rev. Clark B. Olsen, 32, of Berkeley, Calif., and the Rev. Orloff W. Miller, 33, of Boston, were less seriously injured.

They told the police they had been attacked by five men in sports clothes after they had eaten dinner in a Negro restaurant.

The meeting of troopers and demonstrators had been awaited here with dread following the Sunday clash, in which 34 marchers were hurt.

Its peaceful resolution resulted from an arrangement between leaders of the march and the troopers worked out beforehand, with the Federal Government as mediator. The arrangement had face-saving features for both sides.

The demonstrators began their march in the face of a Federal Court injunction prohibiting the march and in spite of a plea against it by President Johnson.

It was clear that the one-mile march was more a gesture than a firm intention to walk all the way to Montgomery. Few of the walkers carried bedrolls or provisions—as many had on Sunday.

After the confrontation, the Negro leaders temporarily suspended plans for any further attempts to make the march, which had been planned to dramatize a struggle to register Negro voters.

Federal District Judge Frank M. Johnson Jr. of Montgomery, who had ordered the Negroes earlier today not to march, will hold a hearing Thursday on a petition by the Negroes to declare unconstitutional an edict by Gov. George C. Wallace banning the Selma-Montgomery march.

Regardless of the outcome of the hearing, the Negroes still plan to hold a demonstration at the Capitol in Montgomery next week to try to present a petition to Governor Wallace pressing the Negroes' voter-registration aims.

At a mass meeting tonight at the Browns Chapel Methodist Church, the Rev. Ralph D. Abernathy announced that a march on the Dallas County Court House in Selma would be held tomorrow. Mr. Abernathy is an aide to Dr. King.

Dr. King told the meeting of the beating of the three white ministers. "Selma had to show its true colors," he said. "It was cowardly work done by night."

Late tonight, University Hospital in Birmingham said Mr. Reeb was in critical condition.

Mr. Olsen, another of the clergymen attacked, is minister of the Berkeley Fellowship of Unitarians. Mr. Miller, the third man beaten, directs college activities for the Unitarian-Universalist Association.

About 450 white persons, most of them clergymen and lay church leaders, had streamed into Selma by airplane, automobile and railroad to join today's march. They came from the North, East and West in response to what they called the brutality of the suppression of Sunday's march.

Fifty white Alabamians who demonstrated here on Saturday on behalf of the Negro campaign returned for today's march.

The White backing encouraged the Negroes in their plans to hold the march and pushed the state government into a greater show of resistance.

More than 100 state troopers, twice as many as were in the force used on Sunday, met the marchers today. There also had been indications that the Alabama National Guard might be called in.

When the confrontation came, the troopers, instead of meeting the marchers with clubs, permitted them to pray in the middle of U.S. Highway 80.

It appeared this morning that the march—which Dr. King had scheduled after the Sunday attempt was blocked—would be called off.

Judge Johnson's order, which had been prepared yesterday and kept secret overnight, was served on the Negro leaders—not including Dr. King—this morning. It ordered the Negroes not to hold their march until he could conduct a hearing Thursday on their petition to overturn the Governor's ban on the march.

Several hundred persons had gathered for the march at the Browns Chapel Methodist Church when the order was announced. They went ahead with their preparations.

John Lewis, chairman of the Student Nonviolent Coordinating Committee, who suffered a skull fracture in the Sunday melee and left the hospital today to go to the church, addressed the crowd.

"On Sunday we saw George Wallace at his best, a vicious system at work," he said. "We have been saying for a long time 'one man, one vote' over requirements to register.

"I understand there's an order from Judge Johnson. I believe we have a constitutional right to march when we get ready, injunction or no injunction."

Other speakers took the same theme. By noon the crowd was bent on marching.

At one point, 3,000 persons were in the area. They filled Browns Chapel, the First Baptist Church a block away and most of the street in between.

There was more a holiday spirit than bitterness in the air, in contrast to the attitude that prevailed on Sunday afternoon as bruised and angry Negroes stumbled back under the lashes and clubs of the officers.

While the crowd gathered at Browns Chapel, Dr. King and his advisers were absent. They spent the morning at the home of a Negro physician, part of the time in conference with LeRoy Collins, director of the Federal Community Relations Service, who had been sent by the President to try to persuade the Negroes not to march.

Cars and buses arrived at Browns Chapel every few minutes bringing more clergymen and out-of-town friends. Some carried sleeping bags and suitcases, but many did not.

Several noted civil rights leaders arrived

with the clergymen. They included James Farmer, national director of the Congress of Racial Equality; James Foreman, executive secretary of the S.N.C.C., and Charles Evers, Mississippi field secretary for the National Association for the Advancement of Colored People.

More than 20 agents of the Federal Bureau of Investigation were reported in the city to watch for any violations of Federal law. Half a dozen lawyers from the Justice Department also were in town.

In the church the Rev. James Bevel, Alabama project director of the Southern Christian Leadership Conference, which Dr. King heads, told the throng that "we are here to announce that we are going to do business today."

Suddenly there was a flurry of movement. Dr. King had arrived. He stepped into the church sanctuary, and as the crowd spotted the Nobel Peace Prize winner it rose to its feet to greet him.

He quickly dispelled a rumor that he had changed his mind and would not lead the march. After expressing appreciation for the out-of-state support, he told the throng:

"We have the right to walk the highways—we have the right to walk to Montgomery if our feet will get us there.

"I have no alternative but to lead a march from this spot to carry our grievances to the seat of Government. I ask you to join me today as we move on."

In 10 minutes they were moving five abreast down Sylvan Street between the red brick apartment buildings of the George Washington Carver Homes.

Dr. King walked arm in arm with Bishop John Wesley Lord of the Methodist Church, from Washington. Near them were A.D. King, Dr. King's brother, and the Rev. Dr. Robert W. Spike, executive director of the Commission on Religion and Race of the National Council of Churches.

Only a few white spectators could be seen, and they were gathered in store doors, staring and saying nothing.

The weather was mild. The street was almost silent as the marchers approached the Edmund Pettus Bridge across the Alabama River.

H. Stanley Fountain, a Federal marshal, stepped in front of the parade as it reached the bridge. He read Judge Johnson's order to the leaders.

Dr. King said they wanted to proceed anyway. Mr. Fountain said:

"I intend in no way to interfere with your movement." He stepped out of the way, and the marchers walked onto the bridge.

Sheriff James G. Clark Jr. drove by slowly and told persons following the parade they would have to have press passes to go any farther. The sheriff was dressed in a brown suit and olive felt hat instead of his officer's uniform, a sign that trouble was not expected.

But the scene was ominous as the marchers reached the crest of the arched bridge. Four hundred yards down the highway could be seen a thick line of blue.

More than 100 troopers stood shoulder to

shoulder, blocking the four-lane highway. Fifty or so troopers and possemen were scattered along the sides of the road.

The marchers grew quieter. When they got to within 100 feet of the troopers, Maj. John Cloud, a state police officer, picked up a microphone and spoke into an amplifying system.

"I am asking you to stop where you are," he said. "We are here to see that this march will not continue."

The marchers stopped 50 feet from the trooper ranks.

Dr. King began to speak, saying the marchers wanted to go to Montgomery to present a petition to the Governor. His words were blurred by a stiff south wind.

"This march will not continue," Major Cloud said, his voice strong and clear on the loudspeaker. "It is not conducive to the safety of this group or to the motoring public."

The troopers stood grimly, each holding a nightstick.

Dr. King said the marchers would like to kneel and pray.

The officer said:

"You can have your prayer and then return to your church if you so desire."

The marchers began singing "We Shall Overcome."

Four of the leaders took turns praying. Major Cloud ordered his men to move out of the highway to the roadsides. Then the road lay flat and open before the marchers. But they made no move to go on.

When the last prayer had ended, the column turned in the highway and headed back toward Browns Chapel.

The marchers sang freedom songs all the way back, beginning with "Ain't Gonna Let Nobody Turn Me 'Round."

JOHNSON SIGNS VOTING RIGHTS BILL, ORDERS IMMEDIATE ENFORCEMENT
By E. W. Kenworthy

WASHINGTON, Aug. 6, 1965—President Johnson signed today the Voting Rights Act of 1965 and announced steps to bring about its quick and vigorous enforcement.

Tomorrow, he said, the Justice Department will officially certify the states where discrimination exists under the definition of the act.

On Monday morning, the President continued, the Justice Department will designate the counties in those states "where past experience" had shown that Federal action was needed to register Negroes.

On Tuesday, he said, Federal examiners will begin registering Negroes "in 10 to 15 counties."

The President also announced that tomorrow at 1 P.M., Attorney General Nicholas deB. Katzenbach would file suit challenging the poll tax of the state of Mississippi on the ground that it is used to abridge the right of Negroes to vote in violation of the 15th Amendment to the Constitution.

Next Tuesday, the President went on, additional suits will be filed against the three other states—Alabama, Texas and Virginia—that require payment of a poll tax as a prerequisite to voting in state and local elections.

The signing took place in the President's Room of the Capitol, just off the Senate chamber. There, 104 years ago today, President Lincoln signed a bill freeing slaves impressed into the service of the Confederacy.

Gathered in the small, ornate room, dominated by a great gilt chandelier, were Vice President Humphrey, the Cabinet, Congressional leaders, members of the Senate and House Judiciary Committees who had refined and strengthened the bill, and Negro and white leaders of the civil rights movement.

Earlier, in the Rotunda of the Capitol, the President said that Congress had acted swiftly in passing the bill and that he intended to act "with equal dispatch" in enforcing it.

In his speech, which was broadcast and televised nationally, the President compressed into three sentences the history, the meaning and the hope of the occasion. He said:

"Today is a triumph for freedom as huge as any victory won on any battlefield.

"Today we strike away the last major shackle of those fierce and ancient bonds.

"Today the Negro story and the American story fuse and blend."

The Voting Rights Act, the President declared, "flows from a clear and simple wrong," and its only purpose "is to right that wrong."

It is nearly five months since the President sent his draft bill to Congress with the adjuration to work "long hours and nights if necessary to pass this bill."

Today the President said that the product of the labors of the Justice Department and Congress was long and complicated.

"But," he added, "the heart of the act is plain."

Wherever states and counties are using literacy tests or other devices to deny the right to vote, the President said, those tests and devices "will be struck down."

And wherever state and local officials persist in discriminating against Negro applicants, "Federal examiners will be sent in to register all eligible voters," he continued.

The states and counties that will be automatically covered by the act are those that have literacy tests and had less than 50 per cent of their voting-age population registered or voting in the Presidential election of 1964.

This formula covers the states of Alabama, Mississippi, Louisiana, Georgia, South Carolina and Virginia, and about 34 counties in North Carolina.

There are more than 2 million unregistered Negroes of voting age in the areas covered by the law. Justice Department officials believe a good portion of these may be registered before next year's general election.

The influx of Negro voters is expected to temper the traditionally conservative tone of Deep South politics because Negroes usually favor welfare legislation and expanded public services.

In areas of the South where Negroes have been registered in large numbers—Atlanta and Memphis, for instance—the effect has been not only to liberalize the political platforms but also to end the traditional contest in racial demagoguery by candidates for office.

The President drove to the Capitol shortly before noon and went first to the office of House Speaker John W. McCormack where the Vice President, Congressional leaders, Cabinet members and prominent civil rights leaders awaited him.

Among the Negro leaders were Roy Wilkins, head of the National Association for the Advancement of Colored People; James Farmer, national director of the Congress of Racial Equality; John Lewis, chairman of the Student Nonviolent Coordinating Committee; and the Rev. Dr. Martin Luther King Jr., president of the Southern Christian Leadership Conference.

Dr. King conceived and led, beginning last January, the voting rights demonstrations in Selma, Ala. It was the club-wielding response of Sheriff James G. Clark Jr., and his deputies—what the President today called "the outrage of Selma"—that spurred the Administration to speed a voting rights bill to Congress.

The President and his invited guests then walked to the Rotunda under the dome of the Capitol.

His lectern had been placed with attention to history and symbol. On his left was the model of Gutzon Borglum's head of Lincoln on Mount Rushmore in South Dakota. On his right was the standing figure of Lincoln by Vinnie Ream. Behind him was the Trumbull painting of Cornwallis's surrender to George Washington at Yorktown.

Behind the President, as he spoke, were the Cabinet, Congressional leaders and his daughter Luci. Before him were gathered members of Congress, the diplomatic corps and other invited guests.

In his speech the President had a special message for those hard-core areas of resistance to Negro suffrage. He said:

"Under this act, if any county in the nation does not want Federal intervention, it need only open its polling places to all people."

But he sounded a note of caution when he said:

"This act is not only a victory for Negro leadership; this act is a great challenge to that leadership. It is a challenge which cannot be met simply by protests and demonstrations. It means that dedicated leaders must work around the clock to teach people their rights and responsibilities and to lead them to exercise those rights and to fulfill those responsibilities and those duties to their country."

Continuing in this vein he told Southern Negroes and their leaders:

"Only the individual Negro can walk through those doors [of the polling place], use that right and transform the vote into an instrument of justice and fulfillment.

"Let me say now to every Negro in this country: You must register. You must vote.

And you must learn, so your choice advances your interest and the interest of the nation."

And he exhorted Negro leaders to remember that they could not meet their challenge simply by demonstrations.

Finally the President had a word both for the North and the South.

While, he said to the North, "there is no room for injustice in the American mansion," there is room for "understanding toward those who see old ways crumbling."

And to the South, he said:

"It must come. It is right that it should come. And when it has, you'll find a burden has been lifted from your shoulders too."

The burden would be lifted from the South, and it would from the nation, because the central fact of American civilization is "freedom, and justice, and the dignity of man," Mr. Johnson declared.

As long as some are oppressed, the President said, belief in these things is blunted and the strength of the nation's high purpose is sapped.

"It is not just a question of guilt, although there is that," he said. "It is that men cannot live with a lie and not be stained by it."

Turning to the future, the President said that the struggle for true equality must move toward a different battlefield, so that the Negro would not merely be secure in his legal rights but be able "to enter the mainstream of American life."

After the speech the President walked to the Senate side of the Capitol and made his way to the President's Room. More than 100 persons crowded in to watch the signing with multiple pens.

The green baize-covered walnut table—known as the "Lincoln table"—that occupies the center of the room had been pushed aside and replaced with a small, simple desk, also covered in green baize.

There is some dispute whether Lincoln used this desk or the "Lincoln table" when he signed the bill freeing slaves forced into the service of the Confederate Army.

But the desk had a personal meaning for the President because it was this desk that he used as majority leader, and it was from this desk that he guided through the Senate the 1957 and 1960 civil rights acts.

Vice President Humphrey was given the first pen, and the Senate Republican leader, Everett McKinley Dirksen, the second.

In this way the President paid tribute to the two men who had played the leading roles in Senate passage of the omnibus Civil Rights Act of 1964. Mr. Dirksen worked closely with Attorney General Katzenbach on drafting the voting rights bill as he had on the civil rights bill.

Among those whom the President invited to witness the signing were Vivian Malone, the first Negro to enter the University of Alabama at Tuscaloosa, and Mrs. Rosa Parks, who started the Montgomery, Ala., bus boycott in 1956. That boycott was the beginning of the Negro protest movement and led to the 1957 Civil Rights Act, the first civil rights legislation since Reconstruction.

SOURCES AND FURTHER READING

Books

The following books were used as reference material for events and specific quotes throughout the book.

Arsenault, Raymond. *Freedom Riders: 1961 and the Struggle for Racial Justice.* New York: Oxford University Press, 2006.

Branch, Taylor. *Parting the Waters: America in the King Years, 1954–1963.* New York: Simon & Schuster, 1989.

Branch, Taylor. *Pillar of Fire.* New York: Simon & Schuster, 1998.

Carson, Clayborne, and Kris Shepard. *A Call to Conscience: The Landmark Speeches of Dr. Martin Luther King, Jr.* New York: IPM (in association with Warner Books), 2001.

Chestnut, J. L., Jr., *Black in Selma: The Uncommon Life of J. L. Chestnut Jr.* Tuscaloosa: University of Alabama Press, 2007.

Cobb, Charles E., Jr., *On the Road to Freedom: A Guided Tour of the Civil Rights Trail.* Chapel Hill, N.C.: Algonquin Books of Chapel Hill, 2008.

Crawford, Vicki L., Jacqueline Anne Rouse, and Barbara Woods, *Women in the Civil Rights Movement: Trailblazers and Torchbearers, 1941–1965.* Brooklyn, NY: Carlson Publishing, 1990.

Hampton, Henry, and Steve Fayer, with Sarah Flynn, *Voices of Freedom: An Oral History of the Civil Rights Movement from the 1950s through the 1980s.* New York: Bantam Books, 1990.

Hunter-Gault, Charlayne, *In My Place.* New York: Vintage Books, 1993.

Jakoubek, Robert E., with Heather Lehr Wagner, *Martin Luther King, Jr.: Civil Rights Leader (Black Americans of Achievement)*. Philadelphia: Chelsea House Publishers, 2005.

Lewis, John, and Michael D'Orso. *Walking with the Wind: A Memoir of the Movement*. New York: Simon & Schuster, 1998.

Trillin, Calvin. *An Education in Georgia: Charlayne Hunter, Hamilton Holmes, and the Integration of the University of Georgia*. Athens: University of Georgia Press, 1964.

Young, Andrew. *An Easy Burden: The Civil Rights Movement and the Transformation of America*. New York: HarperCollins Publishers, 1996.

Speeches and Primary Source Texts

Speeches and texts referenced in this book can be found in their entirety at the following Web sites.

Ross Barnett's Declaration against integration: microsites. jfklibrary.org/olemiss/controversy /doc2.html

Lyndon B. Johnson's State of the Union Address, 1964: www.lbjlib.utexas.edu/johnson/archives .hom/speeches.hom/640108.asp

Lyndon B. Johnson's "We Shall Overcome" speech: www.historyplace.com/speeches/johnson

John F. Kennedy's Civil Rights address: www.jfklibrary.org/JFK/Historic-speeches.aspx

John F. Kennedy's Labor Day Statement: www.presidencyucsb.edu

Martin Luther King, Jr.'s "I have a dream" speech: www.MLKonline.net

Martin Luther King, Jr.'s "Letter from a Birmingham Jail": www.MLKonline.net

Martin Luther King, Jr.'s "Mountaintop" speech: www.MLKonline.net

Barack Obama's inauguration speech: Obamaspeeches.com

Barack Obama's Selma Voting Rights Speech: blogs.suntimes.com/sweet/20071031obamas _selma_speech_text_as_de.html

Barack Obama's statement on race: Obamaspeeches.com

George Wallace's "School House Door" speech: www.archives.state.al.us/govs_list/schooldoor.html

Articles from *The New York Times*

The following articles were used as reference material for events described in the book.

"Excerpts from King's Montgomery Address." *The New York Times,* March 26, 1965.

Hailey, Foster, "Dr. King Arrested at Birmingham." *The New York Times,* April 13, 1963.

Handler, M. S., "Mississippi Faces Drive for Rights." *The New York Times,* May 17, 1964.

Sitton, Claude, "Mississippi Fears Rights Violence." *The New York Times,* May 30, 1964.

Sitton, Claude, "Alabama Admits Negro Students." *The New York Times,* June 12, 1963.

Wicker, Tom, "President Meets March Leaders." *The New York Times,* August 29, 1963.

The following articles appear in their entirety in the Articles section of this book (articles listed in order of appearance).

Nagourney, Adam., "Obama Elected President as Racial Barrier Falls." *The New York Times,* November 5, 2008.

Huston, Luther A., "High Court Bans School Segregation; 9-to-o Decision Grants Time to Comply." *The New York Times,* May 18, 1954.

Sitton, Claude, "Negro Sitdowns Stir Fear of Wider Unrest in South." *The New York Times,* February 15, 1960.

Sitton, Claude, "2 Negro Students Enter Georgia U." *The New York Times,* January 11, 1961.

Lewis, Anthony, "400 U.S. Marshals Sent to Alabama as Montgomery Bus Riots Hurt 20; President Bids State Keep Order." *The New York Times,* May 21, 1961.

Sitton, Claude, "3,000 Troops Put Down Mississippi Rioting and Seize 200 as Negro Attends Classes." *The New York Times,* October 2, 1962.

Kenworthy, E. W. "200,000 March for Civil Rights in Orderly Washington Rally; President Sees Gain for Negro." *The New York Times,* August 29, 1963.

Sitton, Claude, "3 in Rights Drive Reported Missing." *The New York Times,* June 23, 1964.

Reed, Roy. "Dr. King Leads March at Selma; State Police End It Peaceably Under a U.S.-Arranged Accord." *The New York Times,* March 10, 1965.

Kensworthy, E. W. "Johnson Signs Voting Rights Bill, Orders Immediate Enforcement." *The New York Times,* August 7, 1965.

Film

Descriptions of the Greensboro sit-in were drawn from the following video:

Seizing Justice: The Greensboro Four. Documentary: The Smithsonian Channel, 2010.

Web Resources

Civil Rights and Restorative Justice Project: www.northeastern.edu/civilrights

Civil Rights Era Cold Case Initiative: www.fbi.gov/news/stories/2010/march/coldcase_030210

How Race Was Lived in America: A *New York Times* Archive: partners.nytimes.com/library/national/race/past-nyt-index.html

NAACP History: www.naacphistory.org

Southern Poverty Law Center: www.splcenter.org

QUOTATION NOTES

Introduction
"I'm here because," Obama, "Selma Voting Rights Commemoration" speech, March 4, 2007.

1960
"to discuss current events," Hampton, *Voices of Freedom*.

"people started to look," Hampton, Voices of Freedom.

"The help, many of whom were black" Hampton, *Voices of Freedom*.

"Felt invincible fifteen seconds after," *Seizing Justice*.

"I was scared," interview with the author.

"The most practical reason," Hampton, *Voices of Freedom*.

"If one person was taking a severe beating," Hampton, *Voices of Freedom*.

"putting lighted cigarettes down their backs," Hampton, *Voices of Freedom*.

"To go to jail," Hampton, *Voices of Freedom*.

"The movement had a way of reaching inside you," interview with the author.

"started feeling the power of the idea whose time had come," Hampton, *Voices of Freedom*.

"racial problems extended far beyond lunch counters," Hampton, *Voices of Freedom*.

"So we approached the problem very scientifically," interview with the author.

"not in keeping with the ideals of Democracy and Christianity," *An Appeal on Human Rights*.

"We were placed in a big open cell," interview with the author.

QUOTATION NOTES BY CHAPTER

1961

"to provoke the Southern authorities," www.studythepast.com/civil_rights_movement.pdf.

"merely what the Supreme Court," Farmer, *Voices of Freedom*.

"We were prepared to die," www.AndrewYoung.org.

"I have a right to go," Arsenault, *Freedom Riders*.

"barely conscious," Arsenault, *Freedom Riders*.

"supplied the choking victims," Arsenault, *Freedom Riders*.

"in case they were killed," Hampton, *Voices of Freedom*.

"Segregation must be stopped," www.pbs.org/wgbh/annex/eyesontheprize/story.

"Had it not been for President Kennedy," www.AndrewYoung.org.

"This is a testing point," crdl.usg.edu/cgi/crdl?format=_video&query=id%3Augabma_wsbn_351998_cc=1.

"the steel was cold," www.AndrewYoung.org.

"When he saw the pictures," Cobb, *On the Road to Freedom*.

"The next morning, August 29," Branch, *Parting the Waters*.

"One of the guys got behind me," Hampton, *Voices of Freedom*.

"Where the students lead," Branch, *Parting the Waters*.

1962

"Federal authorities alone," www.justice.gov/crt/foia/readingroom/bostonjfk/pdfs/035-umiss-umiss-part1.pdf.

"No school in our State," Barnett, "Declaration to the People of Mississippi," September 13, 1962.

"playing out the last chapter of the Civil War," Hampton, *Voices of Freedom*.

1963

"If you win in Birmingham," Hampton, *Voices of Freedom*.

"spoiling for a fight," Young, *An Easy Burden*.

"probably the most throughly segregated," King, *Letter from a Birmingham Jail*.

"Bevel reminded us" Young, *An Easy Burden*.

"Some have commented," King, *Letter from a Birmingham Jail*.

"The unwelcomed, unwanted, unwarranted," Wallace, "School House Door" speech, June 11, 1963.

"From the outset," Sitton, *The New York Times*, June 12, 1963.

"Never knowing when that bullet," Hampton, *Voices of Freedom*.

"The rights of every man," Kennedy, "Civil Rights Address," June 11, 1963.

"Five score years ago," King, "I Have a Dream" speech, August 28, 1963.

"One cannot help," Wicker, *The New York Times*.

"Accelerate its efforts," Kennedy, "Labor Day Statement," September 4, 1963.

"The apathy and complacency," Hampton, *Voices of Freedom*.

1964

"it would be necessary to bring," Hampton, *Voices of Freedom*.

"I think college students," Handler, *The New York Times*.

"movement for racial justice," Hampton, *Voices of Freedom*.

"As far as I'm concerned," Lewis, *Walking with the Wind*.

"I traveled twenty-six miles," Hampton, *Voices of Freedom*.

"will not only cost you," Branch, *Pillar of Fire*.

"the strongest civil rights speech," Young, *An Easy Burden*.

"Let this session be known," Johnson, "State of the Union Address," January 8, 1964.

1965

"The first struggle," Chestnut, *Black in Selma*.

"[Residents of Selma] were like the dog," Young, *An Easy Burden*.

"You people have been working," Chestnut, *Black in Selma*.

"His eyes were all swollen," Chestnut, *Black in Selma*.

"We must be willing," Jakoubek, *Martin Luther King, Jr.*

"set the stage," Young, *An Easy Burden*.

"It looked like," Chestnut, *Black in Selma*.

"How long will justice be crucified," King, "Our God is Marching On" speech March 25, 1965.

"Our aim must never be," *The New York Times,* March 26, 1965.

"For the cries of pain," Johnson, "We Shall Overcome" speech, March 15, 1965.

ACKNOWLEDGMENTS

As I hope my book makes clear, no one gets to the mountaintop alone. And that is certainly true when it comes to producing this book. I particularly want to thank Alex Ward for being a quiet, but constant shepherd, and my editor, Deirdre Langeland, whose ever encouraging words helped me give birth to the book as she was in the process of giving birth to her baby daughter, Frederica Blythe Geppner, aka Freddie. Maggie Berkvist's enthusiasm for locating photographs to help illustrate the book was also such an inspiration to me. She did a remarkable job with a remarkable spirit.

I also owe a debt to Patricia Sullivan, Professor of History at the University of South Carolina, who herself has chronicled aspects of the movement for civil rights in this country and who took the time not only out of her very demanding writing, teaching, and traveling schedule, but also out of her few days of rest on Martha's Vineyard to read the manuscript and offer valuable insights.

My good friends, Wylma Long Blanding, Carolyn Long Banks, and Julian Bond, who started their journey to the mountaintop at the same time I did, have always been there for me, most notably in this instance with memories that helped stimulate mine. Gratitude also to my first journalist role model, Calvin Trillin, who understood and chronicled the myriad journeys to the mountaintop as they were happening like no other.

And finally, I want to thank my eternally youthful husband, Ronald T. Gault, always my first, most thoughtful reader, who never tires of my demands because he understands.

—Charlayne Hunter-Gault
Martha's Vineyard, Massachusetts, August, 2011

PICTURE CREDITS

INDEX

TURN THE PAGE FOR

A Q&A WITH

CHARLAYNE HUNTER-GAULT

CHARLAYNE HUNTER-GAULT

What did you want to be when you grew up?

My dream was to be like the comic strip character Brenda Starr, whom I got to know as I read the comic strips after my grandmother read the main sections of the paper. Brenda lived a very exciting life covering news all over the world and, even though I lived in a small, segregated town in Georgia, I latched onto her, and her adventures fed my dreams.

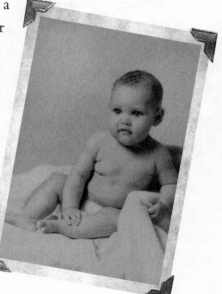

When did you realize you wanted to be a writer?

I started with the dream of becoming a reporter, but once I got to *The New Yorker* magazine after I

Born to dream.

finished college, I saw the possibility of being both a reporter and a writer. So many famous writers, like J. D. Salinger, and reporters, like Calvin Trillin, walked past the desk where I was starting out as an editorial assistant, and their work helped fuel my dreams to be both a reporter and a writer.

What's your most embarrassing childhood memory?

I was fair skinned and had gray eyes and I used to be bullied by a small group of girls. They used to try to push me into fights with other girls. I refused and was made fun of.

What's your favorite childhood memory?

When I was in elementary school, the schools for black children were separate and unequal, often with worn and torn hand-me-down books from the better-resourced white schools. My black school sponsored a

Despite appearances, a tomboy.

fund-raiser each year to help make up for the deficits, and the child of the family that raised the most money would be crowned king or queen. One year, my family raised the most money, and I was crowned queen. I was rewarded with a Bulova watch and a "diamond" tiara. The notion that I was a queen took up residence in my head, and many years later, as I was met with jeers and nasty racial name-calling when I entered the University of Georgia as its first black female student, I looked around for the person they were calling those names because I still thought of myself as The Queen.

As a young person, who did you look up to most?

I looked up to my mother, Althea Brown Hunter. She often read one book a day and was a great letter writer—my father was in the military and served in two wars, so she wrote to him a lot. And when I told her I wanted to be a reporter like Brenda Starr, she didn't tell me that little black girls didn't

A queen again, this time by popular vote.

have a chance to realize that ambition in a segregated society. She simply said: "If that's what you want to do." That's because I think while she had no idea that my generation would defeat the "separate but equal" laws that limited the advancement of African Americans in the South, she also instinctively believed that dreams propel ambition, and she wanted me to have ambition.

What was your favorite thing about school?

I loved the teachers who encouraged me, as my mother did, to follow my dreams. And I started on that path at the Henry McNeal Turner High School in Atlanta as the first eleventh grader to become editor of the school paper, *The Green Light*. I was allowed to leave classes early to go and interview other students and teachers, and I loved having that privilege and freedom. I was not one to sit still.

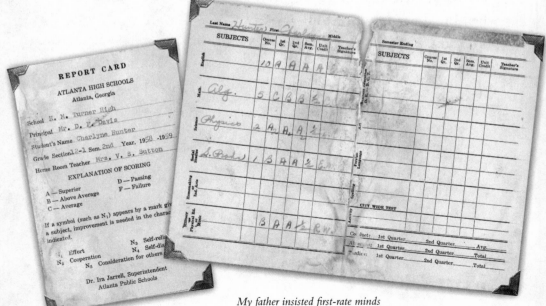

My father insisted first-rate minds don't make Bs, so I stepped up.

*A great group of seniors involved in
many extracurricular activities.*

*Proud Brown Belles dressed
for the Coronation Ball.*

A crowning moment.

Proud escorts of the Queen's Court.

What were your hobbies as a kid?
I didn't have any hobbies other than reading books, if you can call that
a hobby.

What are your hobbies now?
I enjoy collecting art and going to flea markets.

What was your first job, and what was your "worst" job?
My first job was as an editorial assistant at *The New Yorker*. I have
never had a "worst" job, although I didn't like having to get coffee for
the editors when I was an editorial assistant.

What book is on your nightstand now?
Americanah by Chimamanda Ngozi Adichie and *Zealot: The Life and
Times of Jesus of Nazareth* by Reza Aslan.

How did you celebrate publishing your first book?
Bill and Camille Cosby threw me a great book party at their New
York home with lots of great friends of theirs and mine, including
Jacqueline Kennedy, the great African American psychologist Ken-
neth Clark, and my enduring friend, the artist David Driskell, who's
also the Cosbys' curator.

Where do you write your books?
Everywhere. Mostly in my home office, but also on planes during
long trips.

Why did you decide to write *To the Mountaintop*?

I was distressed by the lack of information our younger generation had about the civil rights movement and the challenges that young people like themselves faced and overcame. I wanted to give young people the stories of courage, commitment, and vision—the ammunition to face their own challenges—and help them understand what it takes to survive and conquer. Even in a democracy like ours, it's important to help hold America to her promise of freedom and justice for ALL. It takes awareness and vigilance and involvement. Our younger generation needs to know they CAN make a difference in their own lives and in the lives of their fellow citizens.

How was writing *To the Mountaintop* different from your other journalistic pursuits? Did you find it more difficult or easier to write?

It was a wonderful challenge to re-create the times that I was a part of and a witness to, but a lot of which I had no part in. I had friends on the front lines of the direct action protests, and it was a lot of fun talking to them and getting more background on their lives than I had. There were times when I cried over some of their sacrifices, including death. The hardest part was being personal. I am so used to writing about others. But my editor sent me back my first draft and insisted, so I made the effort.

Even then, big for my age and moody.

**What do you hope readers take away
from reading *To the Mountaintop*?**

I hope readers will appreciate the power
of activism and idealism and never believe that idealism is out of fashion or un-
realistic. The generation I write about
defeated generations of unjust laws and
changed the face of the American
South and, therefore, America in the
eyes of the world. Those young activists also inspired other movements for freedom and justice, particularly in South Africa, and
even most recently the countries of the Arab Spring.

*In elementary school, I
loved the hairstyle of the
hour . . . baby-doll curls.*

**You stress the impact that students can have on history.
Do you think that there is an issue today similar to the civil
rights movement that young people can get behind?**

As President Obama has emphasized, the U.S. Constitution speaks not
of a perfect union but of "a more perfect union," so this generation,
as Frantz Fanon wrote, "must, out of relative obscurity, discover its
mission, fulfill it, or betray it." The choice is theirs, and there are
myriad challenges.

**The civil rights movement has come a long way since 1959.
What do you think is next?**

Despite the election of America's first African American president, we
are not yet in a "postracial society." The goals of the movement are

still calling us, in the words of Dr. Martin Luther King, to judge people not "by the color of their skin but by the content of their character." As we move toward a new demographic in the United States, where the current [white] majority becomes a minority and people of color the majority, we need to continue to stress that ideal and try to make it a reality—not just in America but in what Dr. King called "the global neighborhood."

What challenges do you face in the writing process, and how do you overcome them?
There are a variety of challenges, including not getting distracted (call it discipline) and also having the patience to do the necessary research. I think years of doing that have helped me get better at shutting the door of my mind to things going on around me—and not eating too many sweets when I feel I need an energy boost.

What makes you laugh out loud?
Great satirists like Jon Stewart on *The Daily Show*, and the jokes that friends send me on a daily basis, especially those about getting older.

What do you do on a rainy day?
I read, answer e-mails, and do things around the house that I have neglected.

What's your idea of fun?
I love playing tennis, having small dinner parties with good friends, and dancing with my husband, Ron.

A dear friend of our family made my white leather suit for our big homecoming game.

Crowned homecoming queen all over again.

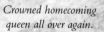

Turner High Wolverine cocaptains Robert Bolton and Hamilton Holmes (my UGA desegregation colleague) present the winning game ball.

What is your favorite word?

You don't want to know.

What was your favorite book when you were a kid?

I don't remember that far back, but the ones I recall the most as a young adult are Ralph Ellison's *Invisible Man*, Zora Neale Hurston's *Their Eyes Were Watching God*, and J. D. Salinger's *Franny and Zooey*.

Do you have a favorite book now?

My favorite book of all time, I think, is *Their Eyes Were Watching God*.

What's the best advice about writing you have ever received?

It was from that legendary editor William Shawn at *The New Yorker*, when I submitted my second short story (he had immediately bought my first, a memoir called "A Hundred-Fifteenth-Between-Lenox-and-Fifth"). And that advice was to lose all but the essentials that helped build the character I was writing about—in this case, my grandmother. I had embellished the story with too many extraneous details. It took me less than an hour to revise it and turn it back in the next day. It was published as "A Trip to Leverton," a fictitious name for Covington, Georgia, the real town I was writing about.

What advice do you wish someone had given you when you were younger?

All my life I had great advice from great people who approached life as that old African proverb goes: It takes a village to raise a child. I had that village in the segregated South and never felt deprived of love and encouragement from that village—my parents, my grandparents, my neighbors, and my teachers at school and Sunday school. So I do not have an answer to this question.

Do you ever get writer's block? What do you do to get back on track?

My writer's block is usually very brief and temporary. And when it happens, I get up from the computer, take a short walk, get a glass of water, run my fingers through my hair, do a few stretches or yoga poses, take deep breaths, and sit back down at the computer.

What would you do if you ever stopped writing?

Not on my horizon.

My baby brother Charles, whom I mothered more than our mother did.

Do you have any strange or funny habits?

Not really, although I have tried unsuccessfully for a number of years to thwart a squirrel from invading the bird feeder outside my living room. I love to take a break from reading or writing to look at the vast array of birds coming to peck at the seeds. So far the squirrel is winning, but I keep refilling the feeder so the birds will still come.

Did you have any funny habits as a kid?

Nope. Unless you count crawling in the red dust under our house in our little Georgia town looking for odd bugs.

What do you consider to be your greatest accomplishment?

Over the years, I have gotten great satisfaction publishing stories of people who have been either overlooked or misportrayed and presenting them in ways that are recognizable to themselves. Giving voice to the voiceless has been one of my greatest satisfactions. Also, getting one of the first interviews with Nelson Mandela and an exclusive with Syrian president Hafez al-Assad.

What do you wish you could do better?

Write a first draft that is the final draft. And being a better doubles partner on the tennis court.

What would your readers be most surprised to learn about you?

That my greatest pleasure comes from being a wife and a mother as well as a professional writer—and striving always to be better at all three. And that I have a shoe fetish.

My 1959 high school senior yearbook picture.